A FIELD GUIDE TO
SHELLS
OF THE FLORIDA COAST

A FIELD GUIDE TO

SHELLS

OF THE FLORIDA COAST

JEAN ANDREWS

Gulf Publishing Company
Houston, Texas

10 9 8 7 6 5 4 3 2 1

Gulf Publishing Company
Book Division
P.O. Box 2608 ☐ Houston, Tx 77252-2608

Library of Congress Cataloging-in-Publication Data

Andrews, Jean.
    A field guide to shells of the Florida coast/by Jean Andrews.
        p.   cm.
    Includes indexes.
    ISBN 0-87719-234-0
    1. Shells—Florida. 2. Shells—Florida—Identification.
  I. Title.
  QL415.F6A48   1994
  594'.0471'09759—dc20   93-28090
                                         CIP

ISBN 0-87719-234-0 (pb)
ISBN 0-88719-249-9 (hb)

Photographs by Jean Andrews and Jean Bowers Gates

Drawings by Jean Andrews

Contents

Introduction

The United States, perhaps the entire Western World, is on a "shell kick." Buyers at the huge markets of the home, gift, and jewelry trades demand and get everything from 18-karat gold snails carrying rock crystal shells or sterling silver nautilus-shaped wine coolers, to paper napkins and bed sheets adorned with a shell motif. Along with these can be seen crates upon crates of the actual shells which have been fashioned into jewelry and home accessories or used as specimens for display. The shell pattern adorning chinaware, glasses, paper goods, calendars, and other products ad infinitum has been designed to suit any taste—good, bad, or indifferent. It has become so commonplace that one might think a manufacturer had been told, "If it doesn't sell, take it back and put a shell on it."

This urge to collect a shell or to employ shell iconography is not a new trend particular to our modern, cosmopolitan society. Archaeologists and anthropologists have made discoveries giving evidence to ancient use of shells not only for utilitarian purposes but also for aesthetic pleasures. There have been periods throughout history when shell collecting has been more "in" than at other times—for example, the century following the end of the Napoleonic Wars (1815–1915)—but it has never been "out." Today, it is IN! Let us hope that contemporary collectors will be guided by good conservation practices in collecting so that future collectors

will be able to satisfy their innate craving for possession of a sea shell.

Shells come in myriad forms and the sea is not their only home. Limitations of space in a pocket guide prevent elaboration on the variety of shells and the reasons for that variety. This has been explained in any number of books that are available to those who would care to go into the subject in greater depth. One of those is the book from which this field guide is derived, *Shells and Shores of Texas*. That book not only provides details about each specimen and the phylum Mollusca as a whole but also contains an extensive bibliography encompassing the literature in the field. Although the history and maps do not relate to Florida, there is a great similarity between the molluscan fauna of the shallow marine waters of the two states.

This guide is intended to be carried to the shore. It concerns the collecting of mollusks from the shallow marine waters of the Florida coast. It includes but a few of those from the deeper waters and none that are to be found on land or in streams, rivers, or bodies of fresh water. It is arranged to help both the novice collector and the professional malacologist identify their finds. No keys have been included, because the method of using this guide is simple. Compare your shell with the photographs in the book until you think you have determined your shell's identity. An illustration of each species is placed beside the descriptions, which are arranged systematically beginning with the most primitive and progressing to the higher orders. When a figure is found that resembles the shape and sculpture of your shell, look first at the size category. If the sizes are not comparable, move on. (See note p. xxii.)

The purpose of a field guide is to make possible the identification of plants or animals in the "field" without additional references, microscopes, or dissecting equipment. Like most field guides, this one may fall short of these objectives but we have tried. If there are terms that are unexplained by the diagrams accompanying the text, we apologize and refer you to the extensive glossary in the "parent" book.

Even those readers who don't know a clam shell from a mangrove seed (both appear on the beach in a gaping posture, but the hard chalky one is the bivalve, the other a dicotelyden) need not be told where to look. A stroll along the beach will reward the sharp-eyed beginner with dead specimens tossed up by the tides. The more seasoned collector will want to gather living specimens. Many mollusks live in the bays in a variety of assemblages—the oyster reef, tidal flats, submerged grass, brackish water, or inlet areas—while others inhabit pilings or jetty rocks, the surf zone, or offshore areas. In Florida the bays and inlets can be rewarding locations, but it will be a fruitless trip unless accompanied by a low tide. Do not attempt it otherwise. Check tide tables and local newspapers; then plan your shelling

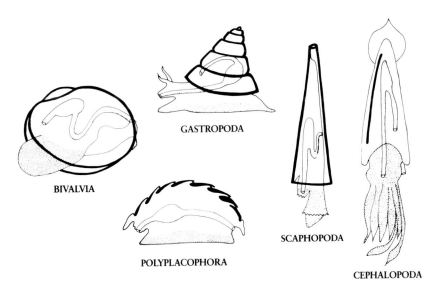

GASTROPODA

BIVALVIA

POLYPLACOPHORA

SCAPHOPODA

CEPHALOPODA

Fig. 1. The molluscan body plan in various classes. The shell is indicated by a heavy line, the digestive tract by small stipples, and the foot by heavier stippling (after R. Buchsbaum, *Animals without Backbones: An Introduction to the Invertebrates* [Chicago: Univ. Chicago Press, 1967]).

expedition to coincide with a minus tide, preferably at full moon following a freeze or cold front.

The "sea shell" is the exoskeleton of animals that constitute the Mollusca, a phylum of invertebrates in the animal kingdom. The habitat of these soft-bodied animals is not limited to the sea, nor is a shell present in all the families that make up this group. Many of the 50,000, more or less, molluscan species do not have shells in either their juvenile or adult stages of development. The slimy slug that plagues the gardener has fantastic counterparts in the sea, the nudibranchs, that far outnumber their shelled relatives. In fact, the absence of an external shell is one of the characteristics of the more highly developed orders of mollusks.

It is virtually impossible to generalize the characteristics of recent mollusks because of the enormous diversity of the members of the phylum. The usual concept of a mollusk is that of an animal with a soft, slippery body and a hard shell, but there are many exceptions, for some, such as the octopus and the sea slug, have no adult shell. However, they all have a soft, fleshy body that is referred to in the name Mollusca, "soft bodied."

The various classes of molluscan animals include chitons that cling to rock; clams that burrow, anchor, or skip; snails that float, dig, or climb; the tooth shell that burrows its wide end into the sand; the jet-propelled octopus that slips through the water leaving a smoke screen of ink in its wake; the primitive, wormlike Aplacophora; and the abyssal-dwelling *Neopilina*. They may be found in any habitat—deserts, trees, rivers, lakes, mud, gardens, coral reefs, the depths of the sea, inside or attached to other animals, and buried in the ground. In all of the animal kingdom their variety is rivaled only by the chordates.

The enormous diversity of the Mollusca makes it difficult to formulate a basic pattern that will apply to all members of the group and still be confined to a brief description. They do have certain biological characteristics that distinguish them from other phyla, but a basic pattern can only be suggested. The unsegmented molluscan body generally contains a variation of three regions: (1) the *head*—sensory-feeding area, (2) the *foot*—locomotor area, and (3) the *visceral hump*—body mass. The tripartite division of the molluscan body is the rule in nearly all mollusks and is not recognizable in any other group of animals. The shell may take many forms or it may be enclosed by the mantle, which is a flap extending from the visceral hump; it may be reduced in size; or it may be completely absent. The shell acts as support or protection for some, but when the shell is nonexistent the animal may develop other means of defense.

Identifying the Shell

One of the most rewarding features of an interest in the field of natural history, whether it be insects, wildflowers, or sea shells, is the pleasure to be had from identifying one's collection. Once collectors are able to name a shell, they can compare their observation of the animal with studies by others. Simply, they can communicate.

Identification of a shell is not always a simple task. A look at illustrations may spot the shell or a near relative so that a reference to the text will point out the real identity. Although the shell of the mollusk may be unsatisfactory as a basis of classification, it is convenient for identification because one seldom has the live animal.

Within a species there might be great variation in color or shape because marine mollusks are extremely responsive to varying environmental conditions. Conversely, some species may be so similar to others that only an anatomical study of the animal will prevent misnomer. Quite often the differences caused by environment are difficult to distinguish from the inherent characteristics of a species.

Standardized names, which can be recognized by students throughout the world, are used to discuss the many kinds of mollusks. Because these names are in international use, Latin or Latinized forms are employed for nomenclature. No one, not even professional malacologists, can remember all of them, but it adds to the pleasure of collecting to be able to recall a few of the more common species.

Like people, a mollusk is given a name of two parts—a binomial. The generic name, always capitalized, is used like the surname, such as Jones or Smith—for example, *Tellina*; the trivial, or specific, name, which is not capitalized and which follows the generic name, corresponds to the first name, such as Jane or George—for example, *texana*. Both of these names are italicized. The name of a person, printed in Roman type, and a date follow the scientific name—for example, *Tellina texana* Dall 1900—indicating the person who first described the species (the author) and the year in which it was described. If the author's name is in parentheses, it indicates that someone has since studied that particular species and placed it in a different genus from that assigned by the original author. If there is a subgeneric name, it is capitalized and placed in parentheses following the generic name. If there is a subspecific name, it follows the specific name without separation by symbol. Thus, *Genus (Subgenus) species subspecies* Author, date.

Many mollusks have common, or popular, names. These names may vary for the same shell according to region, but in most cases they are names in use by local collectors and fishermen. Many small shells are too little known to have been given a common name.

Until recently much molluscan classification was done on the basis of shell characteristics, but contemporary scientific work emphasizes the study of the organism. The result has been reclassification of many species, and the end is not near. Biologists are becoming aware of unique research potentials and amateurs have an increasing interest in studying the mollusk as a living animal.

Amateurs can make a significant contribution to the science of malacology if they would consider the mollusk as a living animal in a particular environment and record their observations. Record and date your observations, making certain your locality data are accurate by including enough information for a complete stranger to locate the spot on a standard map.

Molluscan Classes

Recent evaluation of the interrelationships of the molluscan classes has caused the introduction of three new subphyla—Aculifera, Placophora, and Conchifera—based on the thesis that all living Mollusca are the offspring of three separate lineages stemming from unrecorded pre-Mollusca. Only the last two are of interest to a shell collector. The most conspicuous is the Conchifera, which is composed of the Monoplacophora and its four descendant classes—Gastropoda, Bivalvia, Scaphopoda, and Cephalopoda.

CLASS GASTROPODA: SNAILS

The name Gastropoda means "stomach-footed ones." The gastropod shell, which consists of one unit, is called a univalve. The gastropod is distinct from the other classes of the phylum because of its asymmetrical, spirally coiled, visceral mass and shell. Gastropods are the most diverse group of mollusks. They have adapted for life in both marine and fresh water as well as on land. The primitive forms may browse on algae or minute animals, but others have become scavengers, parasites, and grazers, as well as active carnivorous predators. Adaptations in form probably were based on the requirements of the feeding pattern. Some of the characteristics of the

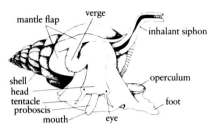

Fig. 2. A coiled gastropod shell with head-foot mass protruded, anterior view (after L. R. Cox, "Gastropoda: General Characteristics of Gastropoda," in *Treatise on Invertebrate Paleontology*, Part I, *Mollusca 1*, ed. R. C. Moore, pp. 184–269 [Boulder, Col.: Geol. Soc. Amer., 1960]; courtesy of the Geological Society of America and the University of Kansas).

gastropods are illustrated in Figs. 2, 3, and 4.

CLASS BIVALVIA: CLAMS

The Bivalvia (Pelecypoda), or "two-valved ones," contain fewer genera and species than the Gastropods, but in number of individuals they may outweigh all other classes of Mollusca and are the most important economically. All bivalves are aquatic filter feeders on detritus and plankton. Their mode of feeding has limited them to strictly aqueous environments, which can be classified into three habitat categories:

1. *Epifaunal,* normally living exposed above the surface of the substratum
2. *Semi-infaunal*
3. *Infaunal,* normally concealed in the substratum

The bivalves invariably have two shells, usually external, on either side of the body. Typically, the two valves are

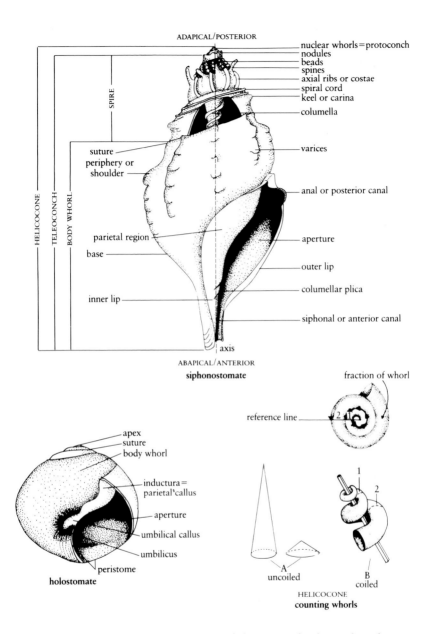

Fig. 3. Parts of the gastropod shell. In this composite shell the columella is seen through a cutaway section. *Counting whorls*: The apical end of the whorl in the diagram is semicircular, with the reference line forming approximate right angles at the sutures. The suture is the line of contact of successive whorls and is perpendicular to the reference line. If there is no coil, there is no whorl, e.g., the limpet. The completion of the first turn is the completion of the first whorl; it does not coincide with the termination of the protoconch. Count counterclockwise from the reference line.

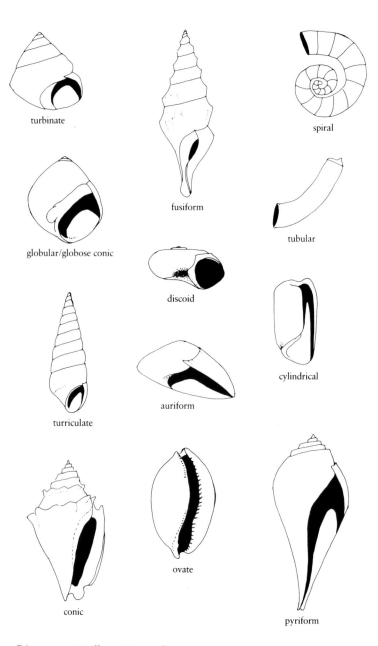

Fig. 4. Diagrammatic illustrations of typical gastropod shell shapes.

of equal convexity (*equivalve*), but in some forms this symmetry has been lost and the valves will differ in size to a varying degree (*inequivalve*). These valves are held together dorsally by a leathery, brown, elastic *ligament*. Some of the characteristics of the bivalves are illustrated in Figs. 5 and 6.

CLASS SCAPHOPODA: TUSKS

The mollusks forming the small class Scaphopoda, "boat footed," burrow with a foot shaped like the prow of a boat. These semi-infaunal marine mollusks feed on detritus and microorganisms with the help of captacula and the foot. The shells are tubular, open at both ends, slightly curved but in one plane, and tapered toward the posterior end. The parts of the scaphopod are shown in Figure 7.

CLASS CEPHALOPODA

The Cephalopoda, or "head-footed ones," are the most highly developed of the phylum Mollusca. These strictly marine animals are found in all the oceans of the world. The Octopoda, octopus, and the Decapoda, squid, are the best known members of this class in Florida waters. Both are carnivores that catch their prey with their numerous arms.

CLASS MONOPLACOPHORA

The Monoplacophora are limpet-shaped mollusks long considered extinct. they are not presently known to occur in the Gulf of Mexico.

SUBPHYLUM ACULIFERA

The Aculifera, vermiform, are marine-dwelling mollusks. These deep-water dwellers have only recently been discovered in the Gulf of Mexico. They are shell-less and very small.

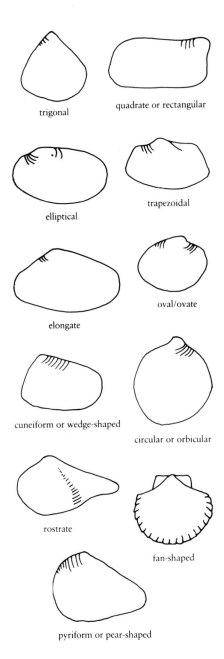

Fig. 5. Diagrammatic illustrations of typical bivalve shell shapes.

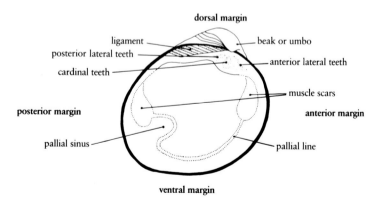

Fig. 6. Parts of the bivalve shell.

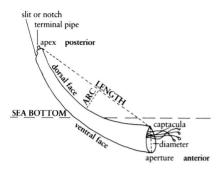

Fig. 7. General features of the Scaphopoda.

SUBPHYLUM PLACOPHORA

The Polyplacophora, or chitons, were formerly grouped with the Monoplacophora in the class Amphineura. The shell has many plates, similar in appearance to that of the garden pill bug. The chiton lives on solid substrata, where it feeds on algae and minute animals. The parts are illustrated in Figure 8.

Data Used in the Descriptions

The basis for the present book is knowledge of molluscan life derived from a long period of field work and continued study of the accumulated information available. Collecting was confined to the shallow-water, or littoral, fauna and included beach specimens and drift material. Smaller species were obtained by picking through algae and sorting drift material with the aid of a stereomiscroscope. No dredging was undertaken. The specimens used to photograph the species that do not occur in Texas were collected in Florida by Theresa Stelsig of Portland, Texas, a member of the Coastal Bend Shell Club in Corpus Christi, Texas, who has done extensive collecting in Florida. David Green, another member who collects in Florida, helped with data on locality and occurrence.

The number of species included in this book in no way implies a complete survey. If the species was collected living, the habitat, together with additional remarks of interest, is given. Many species were not found alive and are indicated as "in beach drift" or "beach shell."

The classification of mollusks is still a matter of debate, and several systems are currently in use. The order used here is basically that of J. Thiele, a standard in the field. The classification of the gastropods is based on a revision in progress by D. W. Taylor and the Siphostomatan [Neogastropod] families of W. F. Ponder. The outline of classification of the bivalves is that of L. McCormick and R.C. Moore. The cephalopods are arranged according to a revision by G. L. Voss.

Some the abbreviations used in the text are cf. (*confer*), compare; ex gr. (*ex*

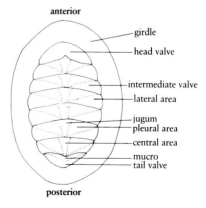

Fig. 8. General features of the Poly-placophora.

Metric System Conversion

Metric			U.S.		
Millimeter (mm)	0.001	m	0.03937	in.	
Centimeter (cm)	0.01	m	0.3937	in.	
Decimeter (dm)	0.1	m	3.937	in.	
Meter (m)	1.0	m	39.37	in.	
Kilometer (km)	1,000.0	m	0.6213	mi.	
Fathom (fm)	1.829 m		6.0	ft.	

grupo), of the group of; s.s. (*sensu stricto*), in the strict sense; sp., species; syn. (synonym), other scientific names that have been applied or may apply; and in litt. (*in litteris*), personal communication. A single capital letter in the generic position of a name represents the genus under discussion.

Listing of synonyms has been avoided unless it was felt there was a need for a reference in order to prevent confusion when making comparisons with other popular shell books or recent changes in taxonomy. If a species was first described in a different generic combination, the author's name and data of publication appear in parentheses, for example (Say, 1922). In some cases, for the sake of clarity, some former combinations are given in brackets, for example [*Cyphoma intermedium*].

The size given is the length of an average specimen. Dimensions are given in the metric scale (1 inch = 25.4 mm; 1 foot = 304.8 mm; see table). The general geographic ranges outside Florida is from both published materials and unpublished records of collectors known to me.

Relative abundance, or occurrence, is given according to the occurrence on the beach and does not reflect the quantity to be found where the mollusks live. *Rare, uncommon, fairly common,* and *common* are the categories used. These are subjective estimates, for there are wide variations, and the use of these categories will serve only as a general guide.

In the prehistoric past the lower Florida Peninsula was separated from the continental United States and the temperate Carolinian Faunal Province was continuous along the continental coast from Cape Hatteras to northern Mexico (approximately latitude 27°N). The more tropical Caribbean Province included all of the Caribbean Sea and much of the Gulf of Mexico with overlapping of the two zones along the coasts of south Texas and northern Mexico. When that Florida gap was closed, the fauna of the Carolinian remained the same but became geographically separated. Consequently, northern Florida, Texas, and the Atlantic coasts of the Carolinas and Georgia have a very similar marine fauna, while south Florida and the southern tip of Texas are Caribbean. Where the two faunal provinces meet there is a certain overlapping of molluscan species.

Florida has such extensive coastal and inland marine water that it is difficult to assign geographic location to the large number of marine mollusks those waters support. Locality is usually designated as south, east, southeast, west, northwest, and entire. These are only guesstimates based on information in *American Seashells*, by R. Tucker Abbott, *Marine Shells of the Western Coast of Florida*, L. M. Perry and J. S. Schwengel, or that furnished by collectors known to me and are to be used only as tentative guides. "Southeast" refers to that area containing shells that range from "Off North Carolina to Florida, Texas, and the West Indies," mostly Caribbean species. "South" includes both coasts from Clearwater on the west to East Melbourne on the East Coast. "Keys" include the area from Miami to Key West; "west" runs from Clearwater on the Gulf of Mexico south to Marco Island; "northwest" is that area from Clearwater north to the Aucilla River in the vicinity of Tallahassee. It is more important to note that shelf marine species will not occur naturally in the enclosed bays; brackish water species will be near river mouths, and so on. Continued study of the coast is broadening these ranges. With few exceptions, the mollusks described inhabit depths of less than thirty meters.

Equipment

Special permits and elaborate equipment are not necessary for collecting on Florida's beaches. The seasoned collector usually has favorite essentials, but the beginner will find the following to be handy:

Canvas shoes: broken shell, bottles, and cans buried in the sand can be a hazard to bare feet.

Long-sleeved shirt and pants: even if a tan is desired, the skin can stand only so much.

Mask, snorkle, and diving gear: to look along the jetties.

Notebook and pencil: to record data.

Pill bottles, vials, small cotton bags: for small and special specimens.

Plastic bags: for collecting drift or wrapping messy material.

Plastic bucket: a light-weight carryall.

Pockets: either built-in or added apron fashion.

Small strainer or wire-bottomed boxes: for sifting shells from sand and mud.

Sun glasses: the glare on the white sand and the water is blinding.

Sun hat: the Florida sun can produce painful burns even on a cloudy day.

Thread or string: to tie valves together.

Trowel: for digging in the sand and mud or lifting the layer of drift from the sand.

Tweezer or toothpicks: to pick up minute shells (wet the end of the toothpick).

Waders, rubber boots, and thermal underwear: since winter brings the best collecting, these items will make the cold fronts bearable.

A friend: collecting alone is not recommended.

Cleaning

Cleaning your shell is of great importance, since a beautiful specimen, improperly preserved, can quickly become an unlovely thing. First, consider the mollusk that is taken alive.

Many types of mollusks may be cleaned by simply boiling them and then removing the soft parts. Start them in cold water with a folded piece of cloth on the bottom of the pan to reduce breakage. Boil or microwave slowly until the flesh is firm or the clam has opened. Cool to lukewarm before washing. Boil only a few shells at a time and remove the bodies immediately when cool enough to handle because cooling causes the body to contract and shrink up into the shell. A corkscrew motion will usually get all the soft parts from the winding snail shell. If the visceral portion of the body breaks off, a few drops of 5 percent formalin (formaldehyde gas dissolved in water) placed in the shell will eliminate bad odors. The formalin should then be removed; no shell should be stored in a solution of formaldehyde, because of the destructive action it has on the shell itself. Dental tools, nut picks, and wires are handy for the body-removing operation.

Some highly polished shells like *Strombus*, *Oliva*, or *Cypraea* will craze if boiled. The animals in porcelaneous shells can be killed by placing them in fresh water. Most can then be picked clean, but some are stubborn. These may be dehydrated in the refrigerator. Wrap each shell in a paper towel with extra thickness next to the aperture and place with the aperture down in the refrigerator for a week. At this time the animal should come out easily. If it does not, do not soak it in anything, for this type of shell waterspots easily. Dry it carefully and allow it to sit with the aperture up until the remaining animal has dried up and can be shaken out.

The true collector wants to preserve the operculum or "trap door" of the operculate shell. Not all snails have an operculum, but they are an interesting feature of many. Mark them in some way so that you keep the correct operculum with its own shell. When these have been dried, they may be glued in their natural position after the thoroughly clean shell has been stuffed with cotton.

Tiny snails are best preserved by allowing them to remain out of water until they die (fresh water will cause them to withdraw far into the shell) and then placing them in a solution of 70 percent ethyl, or grain, alcohol or 50 percent methyl or isopropyl alcohol. If they are placed directly in the alcohol, the animal will contract and draw the operculum into a position where it will not be visible. After several days in the solution the small snail shells may be drained and spread to dry before storing.

The bivalves or clams are cleaned in the same way, taking care not to break the ligament that holds the two sections together. Many collectors prefer that the shell be dried closed in its natural position. After the soft parts are removed, cotton string is wrapped around the closed valves until the ligament dries. Rubber bands, adhesive tape, and other tapes may prove disastrous. Heat causes the rubber to melt and the adhesive coating on the tape comes off, leaving a hard-to-remove residue on the once-beautiful shell. Other collectors prefer that the bivalve be dried in a butterfly position so that the interior is visible. If one is fortunate enough to have several specimens, it is desirable to dry the clam in both positions. William J. Clench, an editor of *Johnsonia,* recommended preserving bivalves in a solution of four parts alcohol and one part glycerine to keep the periostracum and ligament soft and pliable. An occasional dab of glycerine on the ligament will prevent it from becoming brittle.

The fastidious collector may want to clean off all the foreign matter that is attached to the outside of the shell. This again is a matter of taste, as many desire their shells in the natural state with the exterior uncleaned. It is a good idea to have an example of a cleaned and an uncleaned shell in your collection because cleaning often reveals hidden beauty.

A stiff brush is usually enough to do the job of cleaning. Growth that cannot be removed with the brush can often be removed with a sharp pointed instrument, such as an awl, a knife, or a dental tool. The limey deposits can prove quite stubborn and often one must resort to muriatic acid. Experience has proved that this job must be done with running water at hand. The shell is held with forceps and *quickly* dipped into full-strength acid, then immediately held under running water. Extreme caution must be used with this method. The acid is a poison and can burn your skin. Use it only as a last resort. Apertures and delicate parts of the shell can be coated with melted paraffin to protect them from the acid. Shells overcleaned with acid take on an unnatural sheen and can be spotted a yard away in a shell shop. The composition of shells varies; some will withstand the acid and others, like the lion's paw, will dissolve

immediately when put in contact with the powerful caustic. The exterior may also be cleaned with ethyl acetate, a chemical which will not attack the calcium carbonate. It is purchased by the gallon from chemical companies.

Often the shell is covered with vegetation and sponge that can be removed by the use of household chlorine compounds. The chlorine will not dissolve the calcium of the shell as do muriatic acid and formalin, but it does have a tendency to bleach the shell if contact is maintained over too long a period. (A note from experience: extended use of chlorine will dissolve your fingernails.)

The following method is not recommended as an enjoyable pastime, but in some cases it may prove necessary. Delicate shells like the purple sea snail may be cleaned by "watering." Place them overnight in fresh water and then rinse away the fleshy parts. This procedure may need to be repeated several times. A word of warning—change the water daily or more often. The decomposition of the animal's body forms corrosives that dull the surface of the shell if it is allowed to remain in the same water for too long a period.

After the shell is cleaned, its natural luster may be restored by rubbing a thin coating of some type of greasy substance on it. Vegetable fats become sticky with age; it is best to use mineral oil, baby oil, or vaseline. Store oiled shells in closed cabinets to avoid the accumulation of dust on the coated surfaces. Most collectors shudder at the thought of a shell that has been coated with varnish or shellac or overcleaned with acids. Don't kill the shell with kindness. A shell carefully cleaned to preserve its natural beauty can be a joy forever.

A word on traveling with a collection of live caught specimens; you may develop your own method but until you do let me recommend a method learned the hard way. Leave the animal in the shell and wrap the individual shell with newspaper, protecting the lip with extra thickness and stuffing the aperture firmly. If paper towels or tissue are available, they work well for the stuffing. Place the wrapped shell in a plastic bag and tie tightly. Plastic garbage-can liners are good for putting several wrapped specimens together and are stronger than smaller bags. Small specimens may be packed in plastic jars in a 30 percent alcohol solution. Carry the whole mess in a garbage can with a tightly fitting lid and cover the top lightly with plastic before putting the lid on. Plan to bring the materials you will use with you from home. Not every place has newspaper. Decomposition of sea life, especially in the Florida climate, is rapid and odorous. In other words, it will stink quickly.

One trip without proper preparation will be enough. A return trip from the west coast of Mexico was ghastly; even the customs agents passed our car without coming near to examine it, waving us on as quickly as possible.

Preserving

In some instances it may be desirable to relax the animal so that its soft parts are preserved in a lifelike manner without excessive contraction or distortion. Magnesium chloride is the anesthetic most highly recommended for marine animals. Try 75 grams of $MgCl_2$ in a liter of fresh water mixed with an equal volume of sea water. If the animal has not been in the solution for more than twelve hours, it may be revived in normal sea water. However, the most readily available material for relaxing is menthol crystals. A few crystals of menthol are added to the water covering the mollusks in a small bottle. Two or three drops of a saturated solution of menthol in 95 percent alcohol may be used. The specimens should be kept cool and undisturbed while being narcotized. After several hours (6 to 48, depending on the number and size of the animals and the volume of water used), to be sure the specimens are insensitive to strong stimuli, such as probing, one or two should be carefully tested in the killing fluid before the entire lot is transferred. It is well to leave them in the menthol for an hour after they become insensitive to the stimuli. If they are left too long, however, the tissue will deteriorate, making the specimens useless for micromorphological studies. When the snails are fully relaxed, the water should be replaced with 5 percent formalin. After a day or so, they can be transferred to 70 percent alcohol. To preserve color in nudibranchs and other opisthobranchs, use an anti-oxidant (Ionol C.P.-40) 0.3 percent by volume in a solution of 5 percent formalin in sea water. A data label must accompany each lot of cleaned specimens.

Storing

The storing of a sea shell collection presents special problems. Although properly cleaned sea shells do not deteriorate, they to tend to fade in direct sunlight and extreme heat. This feature, combined with their variety of size and shape, makes the shell collection hard to store.

There are several types of collections—the whatnot shelf, the display cabinet, the study collection, the aquarium, and the photograph collection. The first is usually the outcome of a summer's beachcombing by the beginner or it may be an auxiliary to the study collection. The second is generally found in museums, clubs, libraries, and even homes. It is planned for visual appeal, is not overcrowded, is well labeled, has good lighting, and contains choice specimens. The study collection is housed more compactly, with the catalog number, scientific name, date found, and location recorded for each specimen.

In a study collection it is essential to record carefully the depth of water, special conditions, occurrence, substratum, and date when the specimen was secured. A shell that cannot be given a definite locality adds no value to a collection. (Not just "Florida" but "outer beach drift on bar, near causeway at Destin, northwest Florida.")

The importance of locality data cannot be overemphasized. Much of the potentially valuable material I collected as a novice was unwittingly lost to science because of improper or careless locality information. Do not trust your memory—jot it down. Distribution maps of the area in which you are collecting can be made by placing dots on standard maps. Without maps, the locality should be accurate to within a quarter of a mile. An example of the importance of this information—in order to avoid frustrating and time-consuming search—is a paper which cited *Busycon perversum* as being from "Obregón, Mexico." The *International Atlas* showed the only two Obregón's to be inland towns. It was not until much valuable time had elapsed that it was determined that the location cited was intended to refer to the fishing port near the Yucatán Peninsula—Puerto Alvaro Obregón, Tabasco, Mexico.

Small plastic pill bottles and gelatin capsules are handy for storing the smaller specimens and may be obtained in a variety of sizes from your pharmacist. Labels made on biological paper withstand time as well as liquid preservatives. Corrugated paper linings in the storage drawers will prevent small bottles and vials from rolling about. Modular plastic boxes with a plastic container to hold a group of them can be ordered from Althor Products, American Hinge Corp., 946 Danbury Rd., Wilton, CT 06897. This company's catalog illustrates a great many types of plastic containers. The tiny shells are best housed in slides. I prefer the micropaleontological slides with glass covers and metal slide holders that can be ordered from Curtin Matheson Scientific Inc., Labcraft, 9999 Veteran's Memorial Dr., Houston, TX 77038.

Larger specimens can be stored in drawers with small boxes for dividers. Avoid the use of cotton because it clings to rough surfaces and is difficult to remove. A little more trouble but worthwhile is lining the drawers with a thick (dependent on drawer depth and shell thickness) layer of foam designed for gun or camera cases or styrofoam—all others will disintegrate in time. Using an X-acto knife or razor blade, cut a berth to house each individual shell. The drawer is beautiful to look at and chipping is kept to a minimum because the shells never touch each other or jiggle around.

A catalog list in a notebook or a card file is a necessity to prevent the loss of the valuable locality data. You will want to record the precise location, the date, and many other data. The method of collection is important, too. Not all this information can be attached to each shell, hence a numbering system must be used for ease in locating the recorded data. Whatever system is used, you will assign to each shell a specific number. This number can be written in an inconspicuous place on the larger shells with india ink and a fine pen. A Rapidograph-type pen is excellent for this job and for recording in your catalog or notebook. Water will not smear dry india ink. A shell too small to write on can have its number affixed to the slide or container.

I prefer the double-entry type of catalog, but it is only one of many systems. With it, acquisitions are first entered as received, the number is placed on the shell or its container. Separate localities may be indicated by letters that are added to the numbers. The second entry is in an alphabetical listing of the genera. Care must be taken to allow space between the names for future additions. The numbers are entered opposite the individual species but are not consecutive. Use a loose leaf notebook for this catalog.

Note: My *Shells and Shores of Texas*, University of Texas Press, 1977 (*SST*) presents an outline of classification used here in Appendix A, pp. 311–15; charts of the environments of most of the mollusks included here in Appendix E, pp. 318–27; a large glossary on pp. 329–34; and an extensive bibliography relating to shallow water marine mollusks covering the literature up to 1977 on pp. 335–53. Although this book is out of print, it can be found in most libraries.

Shell Condition

Shell collectors who exchange shells or purchase shells like to know what they are getting. A set of international shell-grading standards has been agreed upon to guide such exchanges.

GEM	A perfect specimen of an adult shell. Gastropods have their correct operculum and periostracum. Bivalves have both valves.
FINE	Only minor flaws on an adult shell. Clean, no repairs.
GOOD	May be sub-adult with few flaws, and exhibit the characteristic of the species. Clean.
POOR	A beach specimen. Faded or worn, with some damage.
JUVENILE	Immature.
W/O	With original operculum in gem quality shell. For other categories, an operculum of the same species.
FULL DATA	Detailed information concerning habitat, date of collection, location, collector.
BASIC DATA	Place collected, collector/dealer, year collected.

A FIELD GUIDE TO
SHELLS
OF THE FLORIDA COAST

Phylum MOLLUSCA Cuvier, 1795

Subphylum ACULIFERA Hatscheck, 1891

Class APLACOPHORA Von Ihering, 1876

The members of the class Aplacophora are minute, deep-water organisms without shells that the average collector cannot expect to find, but their recent collection and identification by Granville Treece is such a significant addition to the molluscan fauna of the Gulf of Mexico that they are listed.

Order CHAETODERMATIDA
  Simroth, 1893
Family RIMIFOSSORIDAE
  Salvini-Plawen, 1968

Genus *Scutopus* Salvini-Plawen, 1968

Scutopus ventrolineatus
  Salvini-Plawen, 1968

Family CHAETODERMATIDAE
  Von Ihering, 1876

Genus *Falcidens* Salvini-Plawen, 1968

Flacidens sp.

Family PROCHAETODERMATIDAE
  Salvini-Plawen, 1968

Genus *Prochaetoderma* Thiele, 1902

Prochaetoderma sp.

Class SOLENGASTRES Gegenbaur, 1878

Family PARARRHOPALIDAE
  Salvini-Plawen, 1882

Genus *Pruvotina* Cockerell, 1903

Pruvotina impexa (Pruvot, 1890)

Subphylum PLACOPHORA Von Ihering, 1876

Class POLYPLACOPHORA Blainville, 1816 = [AMPHINEURA Von Ihering, 1876, in part]

Order NEOLORICATA
Bergenhayn, 1955
Suborder ISCHNOCHITONINA
Bergenhayn, 1930
Family ISCHNOCHITONIDAE
Dall, 1889

Genus *Ischnochiton* Gray, 1847

Mesh-Pitted Chiton
Ischnochiton papillosus
(C. B. Adams, 1845)

Size: 8–12 mm.
Color: Whitish, mottled with olive green.
Shape: Oval.
Ornament or sculpture: Girdle narrow, alternately white and olive; upper surfaces of valves sculptured with microscopic pittings; end valves with concentric rows of fine, low beads; lateral areas with fine, sinuous, longitudinal lines; posterior valve concave with 9 slits.
Habitat: High-salinity lagoons on shell and reefs; offshore.
Localities: West; Keys.
Occurrence: Fairly common.
Range: Tampa to lower Keys; Texas; West Indies.
Remarks: Under old shell in bays.

Subfamily CHAETOPLEURINAE
Plate, 1899

Genus *Chaetopleura*
Shuttleworth, 1853

Chaetopleura apiculata (Say, 1839)

Size: 7–20 mm.
Color: Variable from ashy gray or brown to buff; interior white or grayish.
Shape: Oval.
Ornament or sculpture: Dorsum carinate; intermediate valves with well-marked oblique lines separating central area from lateral area which bear numerous rounded beads; girdle narrow, mottled, with scattered transparent hairs.
Habitat: High-salinity lagoons on jetty and reef.
Localities: Entire.
Occurrence: Common.
Range: Cape Cod; both sides of Florida; Texas.
Remarks: More common offshore. Fifth valve broken in figured specimen.

Subphylum CONCHIFERA Gegenbaur, 1878

Class MONOPLACOPHORA Wenz, 1940

To date no member of this class has been found living in the Gulf of Mexico.

Class GASTROPODA Cuvier, 1797

Subclass PROSOBRANCHIA Milne Edwards, 1848 = [STREPTONEURA Spengel, 1881]
Infraclass DIOTOCARDIA Mörch, 1865 = [ARCHAEOGASTROPODA Thiele, 1925]
Order RHIPIDOGLOSSA Mörch, 1865
Suborder ZEUGOBRANCHIA Von Ihering, 1876
Superfamily FISSURELLACEA Fleming, 1822
Family FISSURELLIDAE Fleming, 1822
Subfamily DIODORINAE Odhner, 1932

Range: Bermuda; Maryland to southern half of Florida; Texas; Gulf of Mexico to Quintana Roo; Surinam; Bazil.
Remarks: Algal covering on live specimens makes finding difficult.

Genus *Diodora* Gray, 1821

Keyhole Limpet
Diodora cayenensis (Lamarck, 1822)

Size: 25–51 mm.
Color: Varies from pinkish, whitish, to dark gray; interior white or blue gray, polished.
Shape: Conic, oblong oval; rather thick shell; like coolie hat.
Ornament or sculpture: Orifice keyhole-shaped, just in front of and slightly lower than apex; every fourth rib noticeably larger; ribs crossed by concentric, lamellar ridges.
Aperture: Oval with heavy callus; margins irregularly and finely crenulated; interior smooth.
Habitat: Intertidal to moderately deep water; maily on underside of rocks, jetties; attached epifaunal.
Localities: Entire.
Occurrence: Common.

Genus *Lucapinella* Pilsbry, 1890
File Fleshy Limpet
Lucapinella limatula (Reeve, 1850)

Suborder AZYGOBRANCHIA Spengel,
1881
Superfamily TROCHACEA Rafinesque
1815
Family TROCHIDAE Rafinesque, 1815
Subfamily CALLIOSTOMATINAE Thiele,
1921

Genus *Calliostoma* Swainson, 1840
Subgenus *Kombologion* Clench & Turner,
1960
Sculptured Top-Shell
Calliostoma (Kombologion) euglyptum
(A. Adams, 1854)

Size: 15 mm.
Color: Dull white with brownish mottlings.
Shape: Oblong conic; almost central apical hole.
Ornament or sculpture: Radial ribs alternately large and small; growth lines form concentric lamellations, or scales, as they cross ribs.
Aperture: Large; interior smooth, white, porcelaneous; callus rounded, smooth, with crenulate margins.
Habitat: On rocks, jetties, oyster reefs; attached epifaunal.
Localities: Southeast.
Occurrence: Common.
Range: North Carolina to southern half of Florida; Texas; Yucatán; West Indies; Brazil.
Remarks: Lives entirely underwater.

Size: Height 2.5 cm.
Color: Pinkish brown, often mottled with white.
Shape: Turbinate, apex pointed.
Ornament or sculpture: Seven and one-half whorls, with rounded keel. Periphery of whorls rounded. Spire extended. Anomphalous. 6 large, beaded, spiral cords with smaller, intermediate, weakly beaded cords on each whorl.
Aperture: Subquadrate; outer lip simple and produced at angle from base. Interior nacreous. Columella white, arched near base. Corneous, circular operculum.
Habitat: Offshore to 57.6 meters.
Localities: Southeast; Keys.

Occurrence: Common.
Range: Carolinas to Florida; Texas; Mexico.
Remarks: The young are hatched as crawling snails.

Jujube Top-Shell or Mottled Top-Shell
Calliostoma jujubinum (Gmelin, 1791)

Size: 2.5 cm.
Color: Brown or reddish-brown, often with white blotches near periphery.
Shape: Top-shaped, apex pointed.
Ornament or sculpture: Beaded spiral threads.
Aperture: Simple, quadrate, nacreous.
Habitat: Under rocks on offshore reefs.
Localities: Entire.
Occurrence: Fairly common.
Range: Carolinas to the West Indies; Brazil.
Remarks: Syn. C. *lunatus* Röding, 1798.

Subfamily MONODONTINAE Cossmann, 1916

Genus *Tegula* Lesson, 1835

Smooth Atlantic Tegula
Tegula fasciata (Born, 1778)

Size: Width 12–18 mm.
Color: Background light or reddish brown; mottled with reds, browns, blacks, white; callus and umbilicus white.
Shape: Turbinate.
Ornament or sculpture: 12 postnuclear whorls sculptured with 3 or more fine spiral threads; umbilicus deep, round, smooth.
Aperture: Rounded with 2 teeth at base of columella.
Habitat: On *Thalassia* grass and algae in shallow water; epifaunal.
Localities: South; Keys.
Occurrence: Common.
Range: Southeastern Florida; Texas; Gulf of Mexico to Quintana Roo; Costa Rica; West Indies to Brazil.
Remarks: The shell pictured is badly worn.

Family TURBINIDAE Rafinesque, 1815
Subfamily TURBININAE Rafinesque, 1815

Genus *Turbo*, Linné, 1758

Chestnut Turban
Turbo castanea Gmelin, 1791

Family PHASIANELLIDAE Swainson, 1840

Genus *Tricolia* Risso, 1826

Checkered Pheasant
Tricolia affinis cruenta Robertson, 1958

Size: 6.2 mm.
Color: Background white or pale orange patterned with spiral rows of squarish, dark red spots.
Shape: Inflated, conic.
Ornament or sculpture: 4½ smooth, rounded whorls; apex rounded; suture impressed; umbilicus only a chink.
Aperture: Elongate ovate; columella with thick, white callus; outer lip smooth.
Habitat: Shallow bays on algae; epifaunal.
Localities: Keys.
Occurrence: Fairly common.
Range: Texas; Yucatán to Panama; West Indies; Northern South America; Brazil.
Remarks: This herbivore may be plant specific.

Size: 2.5 cm.
Color: Orangish, greenish, brown, or grayish with flamelike white spits.
Shape: Obliquely ovate; spire conic.
Ornament or sculpture: Strongly beaded spiral threads.
Aperture: White, round; nacreous within. Calcareous operculum.
Habitat: Under rocks, subtidal, rough bottoms.
Localities: Entire?
Occurrence: Common.
Range: Carolinas to the West Indies; Brazil.
Remarks: Red color forms are from deeper water.

Suborder PLANILABIATA Stoliczka, 1868
Superfamily NERITACEA Rafinesque, 1815
Family NERITIDAE Rafinesque, 1815

Genus *Nerita* Linné, 1758

Bleeding Tooth
Nerita peloronta Linné, 1758

Size: 2.5 cm.
Color: Yellowish with red and black zigzag markings. Parietal area stained blood-red with 2 or 3 white teeth.
Shape: Semilunar, solid, with flat columella.
Ornament or sculpture: Coarse spiral threads.
Aperture: White, large, rounded. Calcareous operculum, orange and brown.
Habitat: Under rocks, subtidal, rough bottoms.
Localities: Southeast; Keys.
Occurrence: Common.
Range: Southeast Florida to the West Indies; Bermuda.
Remarks: Those in the Keys are fairly large with good color patterns. Often found with *N. versicolor*.

Four-Toothed Nerite
Nerita versicolor Gmelin, 1791

Size: 2 cm.
Color: Dirty-white, variegated with red and black spots. Parietal area white to yellowish.
Shape: Semilunar, globular, solid, with flat columella.
Ornament or sculpture: Coarse spiral threads throughout.
Aperture: Rounded, parietal area with 4 strong teeth. Calcareous operculum; brownish-gray; papillose above, smooth below; slightly concave.
Habitat: Ocean swept rocks.
Localities: South.
Occurrence: Common.
Range: South Florida to the West Indies; Bermuda.
Remarks: Syn. *N. nigrocincta* Usticke, 1959. Those in the Keys are more colorful.

Checkered Nerite
Nerita tessellata Gmelin, 1791

Antillean Nerite
Nerita fulgurans Gmelin, 1791

Size: 19–25.4 mm.
Color: A black and white checkered pattern.
Shape: Globose conic; body whorl expanded, spire low.
Ornament or sculpture: Coarse, irregular width spiral ridges.
Aperture: Less prominent teeth and not as wide as *N. fulgurans.* Calcareous operculum is black.
Habitat: Under rocks at low tide; intertidal.
Localities: Southeast.
Occurrence: Common.
Range: Florida, West Indies, and Bermuda.
Remarks: Rarely found in northern Florida. Black operculum color separates it from the easily mistaken *N. fulgurans.*

Size: 18–25 mm.
Color: Dark gray to black with occasional blurred markings.
Shape: Globose conic; body whorl expanded, spire low.
Ornament or sculpture: Strong spiral cords; heavy shell.
Aperture: Large, rounded with 2 prominent teeth on inside of outer lip; inner lip yellowish white, toothed, with decklike, porcelaneous callus.
Habitat: Marine; jetties and pilings near high-tide mark; epifaunal.
Localities: Entire.
Occurrence: Common.
Range: Southeastern Florida; Texas; Yucatán; Costa Rica; West Indies; northeastern Brazil.
Remarks: Can live around 75 days out of water. Places eggs on own shell or those of other mollusks.

Genus *Neritina* Lamarck, 1816
Subgenus *Vitta* Mörch, 1852

Olive Nerite
Neritina (Vitta) reclivata (Say, 1822)
[See *SST*, p. 75]

Virgin Nerite
Neritina (Vitta) virginea (Linné, 1758)

Size: 4–12 mm.
Color: Color and pattern variable: background olive, white, gray, red, yellow, purple, or black with black and/or white waves, stripes, dots, lines, or mottlings.
Shape: Globular with expanded body whorl.
Ornament or sculpture: Smooth, polished.
Aperture: Semilunar; parietal area smooth, convex, white to yellow, with variable number of small, irregular teeth.
Habitat: Bay margins and grass flats; epifaunal.
Localities: Entire.
Occurrence: Common.
Range: Bermuda; Florida to Texas; Gulf of Mexico to Quintana Roo; Costa Rica; West Indies; Surinam; almost all of Brazilian coast.
Remarks: Lays eggs in winter on own shell or that of other mollusks; eggs are in clustered, yellowish, gelatinous capsules; patterns so varied one might think each a different species; more colorful in brackish water than in more saline water; photosensitive.

Genus *Smaragdia* (Maury, 1917)

Emerald Nerite
Smaragdia viridis viridemaris (Maury, 1917)

Size: 6–16 mm.
Color: Bright pea green with few fine, broken white lines near apex; these outlined in maroon color in some specimens.
Shape: Obliquely oval, subglobular, low spire.
Ornament or sculpture: Glossy, smooth.
Aperture: Simple, semilunar; outer lip thin, sharp; parietal area green with 7 to 9 minute teeth.
Habitat: Grass flats in shallow bays; epifaunal.
Localities: Port Aransas, south.
Occurrence: Uncommon.
Range: Bermuda; southeastern Florida; Texas; Gulf of Mexico to Quintana Roo; Costa Rica; West Indies.
Remarks: Animal green; photosensitive; first reported living in Texas by me.

Infraclass MONOTOCARDIA Mörch, 1865 = [CAENOGASTROPODA Cox, 1959]
Order CTENOBRANCHIA Schweigger, 1820 = [PECTINIBRANCHIA Blainville, 1814]
Suborder HOLOSTOMATA Fleming, 1828
Superfamily LITTORINACEA Gray, 1840

Family LITTORINIDAE Gray, 1840
Subfamily LITTORININAE Gray, 1840

Genus *Littorina* Férussac, 1821
Zebra Periwinkle
Littorina ziczac (Gmelin, 1791)

Subgenus *Littorinopsis* Mörch, 1876
Angulate Periwinkle
Littorina (Littorinopsis) angulifera
  (Lamarck, 1822)

Size: 1.3 cm.
Color: Whitish, with dark brown or black wavy stripes.
Shape: Ovately conical.
Ornament or sculpture: Fine, widely spaced spiral groves.
Aperture: Oval and small; operculum chitinous.
Habitat: Intertidal zone in rock crevices.
Localities: Southeast.
Occurrence: Common.
Range: South Florida to the West Indies; Bermuda. Introduced to Pacific Panama.
Remarks: Often confused with L. *lineolata* Orbigny, 1840.

Size: 25–30 mm.
Color: Background varies: bluish white, orange yellow, dull yellow, reddish brown, or grayish brown.
Shape: Conic with elongate spire; higher than wide.
Ornament or sculpture: Darker elongated spots on ribs, often fused to form oblique stripes on body whorl; early whorls have regularly spaced, vertical white spots below suture; about 6 convex whorls, body whorl about one-half of height; slightly channeled sutures; spiral sculpture of irregular, inequidistant incised lines; anomphalous.
Aperture: Rounded oval; outer lip smooth, does not flare, sharp and nearly horizontal at body whorl; inner lip with thin deposit over body whorl; columellar area smooth, moderately wide, with central groove in lower portion.
Habitat: Brackish water; mangrove thickets, on black mangrove, *Avicennia nitida* (subject to freeze in this area); climbs high into tree and can spend much time out of water; at times on pilings and rocks; epifaunal.
Localities: Entire.
Occurrence: Common.
Range: Bermuda; southern half of Florida; Texas; West Indies; Brazil.; Pacific Panama; central west Africa.

Remarks: After hard freezes this species disappears.

Marsh Periwinkle
Littorina (Littorinopsis) irrorata (Say, 1822)

Size: 25 mm.
Color: Grayish white with tiny, short streaks of reddish brown on spiral ridges; opaque, dull.
Shape: Elongate conic; longer than wide.
Ornament or sculpture: 8 to 10 gradually increasing, flat whorls; suture weak; body whorl about one-half of total height; numerous, regularly shaped spiral grooves; shell thick.
Aperture: Oval; columella and callus usually pale reddish brown; outer lip stout, sharp, with tiny, regular grooves on inside edge.
Habitat: On marsh grass in low-salinity bays; epifaunal.
Localities: Entire.
Occurrence: Common.
Range: New Jersey to central Florida to Texas.
Remarks: Herbivorous on algae; when tide out, animal withdraws into shell, which may remain dry and exposed to sun for many hours; often completely out of water on stems of marsh grass where it leaves a mucus trail.

Subgenus *Austrolittorina* Rosewater, 1970

Lineolate Periwinkle
Littorina (Austrolittorina) lineolata Orbigny, 1840

Size: 12–25 mm.
Color: Background gray with oblique zigzag lines of dark brown; apex reddish brown.
Shape: Elongate conic.
Ornament or sculpture: 6 to 8 gradually increasing convex whorls; body whorl more than one-half of total height, more convex than other whorls; suture well marked; male smaller and more strongly sculptured with spiral grooves than female.
Aperture: Pear-shaped; outer lip not flaring, edge sharp and thin; meets body whorl at sharp angle; columellar area long, wide, slanting inward, smooth; anomphalous; purple to mahogany brown.
Habitat: Intertidal on rocks, jetties, pilings; often in large colonies in crevices; epifaunal.
Localities: South.
Occurrence: Common.
Range: Bermuda; southern half of Florida to Texas; Costa Rica; Brazil.
Remarks: Often has been misidentified as *L. ziczac* (Gmelin, 1790). *L. lineolata* darker in color, smaller, and with a wider apical angle.

Subgenus *Littoraria* Gray, 1834

Cloudy Periwinkle
Littorina (Littoraria) nebulosa
(Lamarck, 1822)

Remarks: Prefers wooden jetties, wreckage, and logs; avoids rocks exposed to heavy surf; seldom survives freezing winters.

Subgenus *Melarhaphe* Menke, 1828

Spotted Periwinkle
Littorina (Melarhaphe) meleagris (Potiez & Michaud, 1838) [See *SST*, p. 80]

Subfamily TECTARIINAE Rosewater, 1970

Genus *Tectarius* Valenciennes, 1833

Beaded Periwinkle
Tectarius muricatus (Linné, 1758)

Size: 15 mm.
Color: Background bone yellow or white with bluish tinge; early whorls have spotting of white and reddish brown, which stops abruptly on sixth or seventh whorl; variable in juveniles.
Shape: Elongate conic.
Ornament or sculpture: 7 to 9 gradually increasing convex whorls; body whorl about two-thirds of total height; nuclear whorls usually eroded in adults; suture well marked, smooth or slightly crenulate behind outer lip; spiral engraved lines become evident on fourth whorl, becoming numerous and more regularly spaced on body whorl; strong transverse striations cross spiral lines at angles.
Aperture: Subcircular; outer lip not flaring; edge thin, sharp, smooth, meeting body whorl at sharp angle; slight callus over body whorl, columella long, wide, smooth; anomphalous; mouth yellowish brown to pale purplish within; outer lip whitish; columella white.
Habitat: Pilings and jetties in more saline waters; epifaunal.
Localities: Southeast.
Occurrence: Common.
Range: Bermuda; Texas; Caribbean coast of Central America; West Indies; northern South America; Pacific Panama.

Size: 2 cm.
Color: Whitish gray.
Shape: Conical, thick.
Ornament or sculpture: Rows of rounded, evenly spaced nodules spiral around the body whorl.
Aperture: Ovate, interior dark-tan; operculum chitinous, dark-brown, paucispiral.
Habitat: Tidal shores on rock above high-tide line.
Localities: South.
Occurrence: Common.
Range: South Florida to the West Indies; Bermuda.

Superfamily RISSOACEA Gray, 1847
Family RISSOIDAE Gray, 1847
Subfamily RISSOINAE Gray, 1847

Genus *Swartziella* Nevil, 1884
Catesby's Risso
Swartziella catesbyana Orbigny, 1842

Genus *Zebina* H. & A. Adams, 1854
Smooth Risso
Zebina browniana (Orbigny, 1842)

Size: 3–5 mm.
Color: Shiny white.
Shape: Elongate conic.
Ornament or sculpture: 8 whorls, slightly rounded; suture fairly deep; about 14 strong ribs to each whorl.
Aperture: Oval, slightly oblique; strong tooth on inner side of outer lip.
Habitat: *Thalassia* grass beds in brackish, shallow, inshore waters; epifaunal.
Localities: Southeast.
Occurrence: Fairly common.
Range: Bermuda; North Carolina; Florida; Texas; Gulf of Campeche; Campche Bank; Quintana Roo; Costa Rica; West Indies; Brazil.
Remarks: Pronounced "riss-o-ee-na"; *R. chesneli* Michaud, 1830, of authors. [*Rissoina. chesneli* Michaud, 1830, of authors].

Size: 4 mm.
Color: Shiny white or pale amber.
Shape: Elongate conic.
Ornament or sculpture: 9 to 10 slightly convex whorls, smooth; suture shallow; apex small, prominent.
Aperture: Oval, entire; outer lip thickened
Habitat: Under shell and debris in grassy bottom beyond littoral zone; epifaunal.
Localities: Southeast.
Occurrence: Fairly common.
Range: Bermuda; North Carolina to Gulf of Mexico; Texas to Quintana Roo; Costa Rica; West Indies.
Remarks: *Syn. Rissoina laevigata* (C. B. Adams, 1850); [*R. browniana*].

Family ASSIMINEIDAE H. & A. Adams, 1856

Genus *Assiminea* Fleming, 1828

Assiminea cf. *A. succinea* Pfeiffer, 1840

Family TRUNCATELLIDAE Gray, 1840
Subfamily TRUNCATELLINAE Gray, 1840

Genus *Truncatella* Risso, 1826

Truncatella caribaeensis Reeve, 1842

Size: 5 mm.
Color: Pale brown, translucent.
Shape: Conic.
Ornament or sculpture: No ornament other than microscopic striae; 5 to 5¾ whorls; regularly rounded, sutures shallow.
Aperture: Pyriform, simple; inductura overlaps preceding whorl; anomphalous.
Habitat: Salt marshes with moisture and protection from sun; lives just out of water; epifaunal.
Localities: Southeast.
Occurrence: Common.
Range: Boston to Texas; Quintana Roo; Brazil.
Remarks: Look for it on sand flats.

Size: 5.5–7.5 mm.
Color: White to pale amber, shiny.
Shape: Elongate conic.
Ornament or sculpture: 4 to 4½ convex whorls; deeply impressed suture; 17 or more poorly developed transverse costae, some specimens may be nearly smooth; costae appear only on upper part of whorl; mature specimens appear very different from young due to loss of early whorls.
Aperture: Ovate, somewhat flaring, entire; angled above and rounded below; outer lip simple, thin, thickened at union with body whorl; columella not apparent; anomphalous.
Habitat: In bays above high-tide and inlet areas; epifaunal but under wet debris.
Localities: Southeast.
Occurrence: Fairly common.
Range: Bermuda; southeastern United States; Texas; Carmen, Campeche, Mexico; Gulf of Campeche; Quintana Roo; West Indies; northeastern Brazil.
Remarks: Formerly misidentified in Texas as *T. pulchella* Pfeiffer, 1839; out of water in damp spots under driftwood along bay margins.

Family VITRINELLIDAE Bush, 1897

Genus *Vitrinella* C. B. Adams, 1850

Vitrinella cf. floridana Pilsbry & McGinty, 1946

Helix Vitrinella
Vitrinella helicoidea C. B. Adams, 1850 [See *SST*, p. 86]

Genus *Cyclostremiscus* Pilsbry & Olsson, 1945
Subgenus *Ponocyclus* Pilsbry, 1953

Jeanne's Vitrinella
Cyclostremiscus (Ponocyclus) jeaneae Pilsbry & McGinty, 1946 [See *SST*, p. 87]

Trilix Vitrinella
Cyclostremiscus (Ponocyclus) pentagonus (Gabb, 1873) [See *SST*, p. 88]

Cyclostremiscus (Ponocyclus) suppressus (Dall, 1889) [See *SST*, p. 88]

Genus *Anticlimax* Pilsbry & McGinty, 1946
Subgenus *Subclimax* Pilsbry & Olsson, 1950

Anticlimax (Subclimax) pilsbryi (McGinty, 1945)

Size: 1.8 mm.
Color: White.
Shape: Slightly turbinate.
Ornament or sculpture: Umbilicus broadly open; protoconch slightly elevated; 2 postnuclear whorls; prior whorls can be seen; walls convex.
Aperture: Circular, oblique; columella slightly thickened.
Habitat: Inlet-influenced areas and near shore; epifaunal.
Localities: South.
Occurrence: Fairly common in beach drift.
Range: Southern Florida and Texas to Campeche Bank; Quintana Roo.
Remarks: Uncarinated umbilicus differentiates this from *V. helicoidea*. [Figures in *SST*, p. 86, are of two different specimens of *V. floridana*.]

Size: 3.4 mm.
Color: White.

Shape: Discoid, spire slightly dome-shaped.

Ornament or sculpture: 2½ postnuclear whorls sculptured with numerous, fine zigzag spiral grooves; more grooves on dorsal side than on base; periphery just above base marked with strong keel; umbilicus partly filled with heavy callus, may be entirely filled.

Aperture: Oblique; lip slightly thickened in adults; parietal callus thick, on preceding whorl.

Habitat: On muddy botton in shallow water; shore; epifaunal.

Localities: South.

Occurrence: Uncommon to rare.

Range: Southern Florida; Texas; Quintana Roo.

Remarks: Callus-filled umbilicus causes confusion with the *Teinostoma*; look for zigzag grooving.

Genus *Parviturboides* Pilsbry & McGinty, 1950

? Parviturboides interruptus (C. B. Adams, 1850) [See *SST*, p. 90]

Genus *Solariorbis* Conrad, 1865
Subgenus *Solariorbis* s.s.

Solariorbis (Solariorbis) blakei Rehder, 1944

Size: 1.45 mm.

Color: White.

Shape: Discoid.

Ornament or sculpture: 1½ postnuclear whorls sculptured with microscopic spiral grooves and brief transverse wrinkles fanning from suture; suture only slightly impressed; nuclear whorls project slightly; base broad, smooth, evenly rounded; umbilicus may be nearly or entirely closed but always a narrow chink and never looks like *Teinostoma*.

Aperture: Oblique, rounded; parietal callus extends beyond apertue.

Habitat: Inlets and bays; epifaunal.

Localities: South.

Occurrence: Uncommon.

Range: Eastern coast of United States; Florida; Gulf states; Mexico.

Remarks: Thickening around umbilicus most distinctive characteristic of genus. [Specimens figured in *SST*, p. 90, are *Vitrinella floridana* Pilsbry & McGinty, 1946.]

Solariorbis (Solariorbis) infracarinata Gabb, 1881 [See *SST*, p. 91]

Genus *Pleuromalaxis* Pilsbry & McGinty, 1945

Bales' False Dial

Pleuromalaxis balesi Pilsbry & McGinty, 1945 [See *SST*, p. 93]

Subfamily TEINOSTOMATINAE Cossmann, 1917

Genus *Pseudorotella* Fischer, 1987

Tiny-Calloused Teinostoma

Pseudorotella parvicallum Pilsbry & McGinty, 1945 [See SST, p. 94]

Genus *Teinostoma* H. & A. Adams, 1854

Teinostoma cf. *bicaynesne* Pilsbry & McGinty, 1945 [See *SST*, p. 93]

Family CAECIDAE Gray, 1850

Genus *Caecum* Fleming, 1813
Subgenus *Micranellum* Bartsch, 1920

Beautiful Little Caecum
Caecum (Micranellum) pulchellum
(Stimpson, 1851) [See *SST*, p. 95]

Subgenus *Elephantulum* Carpenter, 1857

Cooper's Caecum
Caecum (Elephantulum) imbricatum
Carpenter, 1858

Size: 4⁻5 cm.
Color: Glossy, opaque, white.
Shape: Curved, tubular.
Ornament or sculpture: Longitudinal
sculpture of about 24 rounded ribs crossed
by numerous rings; more prominent near
aperture, giving cancellate appearance;
apical plug has prong to one side; fairly
heavy shell.
Aperture: Round.
Habitat: Offshore on sand and shell banks.
Localities: Entire.
Occurrence: Common.
Range: South of Cape Cod to northern
Florida and Texas; Campeche Bank;
Quintana Roo; Bahamas; West Indies.
Remarks: Syn. *C. cooperi* (S. Smith, 1870);
most caecums feed on diatoms and detrital
particles in algal thickets in well-lighted
zones on rocks, gravel, sand, and mud.

Subgenus *Brochina* Gray, 1857

Johnson's Caecum
Caecum (Brochina) johnsoni Winkley,
1908

Size: 4.5 mm.
Color: White.
Shape: Curved, tubular.
Ornament or sculpture: Shell narrow, thin,
smooth, subdiaphanous; aperture not
contracted or tumid, white; septum without
appendage.
Aperture: Circular, not constricted.
Habitat: Bays and oyster reefs; epifaunal.
Localities: Entire.
Occurrence: Common in beach drift.
Range: Europe; North Carolina to Florida;
Texas.

Remarks: Lay eggs in capsules attached to bottom; often confused with *C. glabrum* Montagu, 1803, a European species.

Subgenus *Meioceras* Carpenter, 1858

Little Horn Caecum
Caecum (Meioceras) nitidum Stimpson, 1851

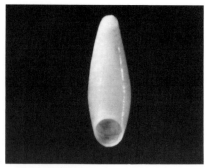

(adult, third stage)

Size: 2.5 mm.
Color: Shiny white or brownish with irregular mottlings of opaque white.
Shape: Tubular with swollen center.
Ornament or sculpture: Smooth, polished; apical plug convexly rounded with tiny projection to one side.
Aperture: Round, oblique, sharp edged; larger than apical end.
Habitat: Intertidal; epifaunal.
Localities: South.
Occurrence: Uncommon.
Range: Southern half of Florida; Texas; Quintana Roo; West Indies; northeastern Brazil.
Remarks: According to D. R. Moore (in litt.), the center figure shows the second and third stages of growth after the protoconch drops off: "The second stage usually drops off when the third stage is about half grown. However, in some areas, especially Aransas Bay, the second stage is retained with all three stages. The septum that seals the posterior end of the shell forms before drop-off. After the septum is formed, the poorly calcified line that marks the separation point is no longer in contact with living tissue. This area then begins to deteriorate and allows separation of the two stages."

(protoconch, first stage)

(second and third stages still joined)

Superfamily TORNACEA Kuroda, Habe,
& Oyama, 1971
Family TORNIDAE Sacco, 1896

Genus *Macromphalina* Cossmann, 1888
Macromphalina palmalitoris Pilsbry &
McGinty, 1950 [See *SST*, p. 97]

Genus *Cochliolepis* Stimpson, 1858
Cochliolepis parasitica Stimpson, 1858

Localities: Entire, more to south.
Occurrence: Fairly common.
Range: Beaufort, North Carolina;
Charleston, South Carolina; western coast
of Florida; Texas.
Remarks: Heavy growth lines give nautiloid
appearance; animal red; syn. *C.
nautiliformis* (Holmes 1860); herbivore, or
detritus feeder, which lives commensally
with tube worm *Polydontes lupina.*

Cochliolepis striata Dall, 1889

Size: 3.55 mm.
Color: White, glassy.
Shape: Discoid.
Ornament or sculpture: 2 postnuclear
whorls smooth except for occasional
growth line; spire flat and partially covered
with thin callus of shell from each
successive whorl; umbilicus shallow,
broadly open.
Aperture: Oblique; lip incomplete; parietal
callus thin.
Habitat: Shallow coastal bay; commensal
with worm; epifaunal.

Size: 6.5 mm.
Color: White.
Shape: Discoid.
Ornament or sculpture: Thin shell has 4
whorls sculptured with numerous spiral
striations; base smooth, but umbilicus
striated; first nuclear whorl slightly
projecting, while remainder covered by thin
callus from succeeding whorls; umbilicus
slightly constricted.
Aperture: Oblique; lip thin, incomplete; no
parietal callus.

Habitat: Shallow coastal bays; probably commensal with a worm; epifaunal.
Localities: Entire.
Occurrence: Fairly common.
Range: North Carolina to Caribbean; western coast of Florida; Texas.
Remarks: Will probably be reclassified into another family and genus.

Superfamily ARCHITECTONICACEA
  Gray, 1850
Family ARCHITECTONICIDAE
  Gray, 1850

Genus *Heliacus* Orbigny, 1842

Orbigny's Sundial
Heliacus bisulcata (Orbigny, 1842)
[See *STT*, p. 99]

Genus *Architectonica* Röding, 1798

Common Sundial
Architectonica nobilis (Röding, 1798)

Shape: broadly conic; spire low.
Ornament or sculpture: Early whorls marked with spiral cords that appear beaded due to growth lines of spire; 4 or 5 prominent sulcations and traces of others on remaining whorls; base flat, more strongly sculptured than topside; umbilicus deep, wide, surrounded with strongly crenulated spiral cord.
Aperture: Subquadrate; lip thin, irregularly crenulated; interior white.
Habitat: Along shore with sea pansies; epifaunal.
Localities: Entire.
Occurrence: Fairly common after storms.
Range: Southeastern United States to West Indies; Texas; Campeche Bank; Surinam; all of Brazilian coast; western Mexico to Peru; eastern Pacific.
Remarks: Miocene species that survives on both sides of Panama; syn. *A granulata* (Lamarck, 1816); usually buried shallowly in sand with adapical part pointing into sand, opposite to most prosobranchs; nocturnal, feeding on soft-bodied actinian-type coelenterates.

Superfamily TURRITELLACEA
  Woodward, 1851
Family VERMETIDAE Rafinesque, 1815
Subfamily VERMICULARIINAE
  Kimoshita, 1932

Genus *Vermicularia* Lamarck, 1799

West Indian Worm Shell
Vermicularia cf. *V. spirata* Philippi, 1836

Size: 25–51 mm.
Color: Background cream with orange brown spots spirally arranged, more prominent next to suture; porcelaneous.

Size: 18–25 mm.
Color: Light brown, paler toward aperture.
Shape: Very elongate conic or turriculate.
Ornament or sculpture: About 6 regular whorls closely coiled; later whorls detached, giving a wormlike appearance; about 3 spiral cords form keels at sutures of later whorls; weak, irregular transverse growth lines; fine spiral threads between major cords.
Aperture: Round, thin lipped.
Habitat: Intertidal, attached to rocks, in mud, in bays; attached epifaunal.
Localities: West.
Occurrence: Common.
Range: Southeastern Florida; Texas; Carmen, Campeche, Mexico; Yucatán; Quintana Roo; Caribbean.
Remarks: The long, coiling shell looks like the calcareous tube of some marine worms.
Syn. *V. fargoi* Olsson, 1951.

Superfamily CERITHIACEA Fleming, 1822
Family MODULIDAE Fischer, 1884

Genus *Modulus* Gray, 1842
Atlantic Modulus
Modulus modulus (Linné, 1758)

Size: Height 12 mm.
Color: Grayish white spotted with brown.
Shape: Turbinate.
Ornament or sculpture: About 3 small whorls in spire; body whorl large with sloping shoulders and keeled base; upper portion of shell marked with low spiral

ridges and oblique, transverse growth lines; five strong cords on base; umbilicus deep, small.
Aperture: Round with thin, slightly crenulated outer lip that is thickened and marked with low ridges within; white, porcelaneous; columella short with distinctive single tooth near base.
Habitat: On *Thalassia* grass; intertidal; epifaunal.
Localities: Entire.
Occurrence: Common in beach drift.
Range: Bermuda; Florida Keys to West Indies; Texas; Gulf of Mexico to Quintana Roo; Costa Rica; almost all of Brazilian coast.
Remarks: Pictured specimen is badly worn.

Family CERITHIIDAE Fleming, 1822
Subfamily CERITHIINAE Fleming, 1822

Genus *Cerithium* Bruguière, 1789
Stocky Cerith
Cerithium litteratum (Born, 1778)

Size: 2.5 × 1.3 cm.
Color: Whitish with rows of squarish black or red dots.
Shape: Elongate cone, pointed apex, stout.
Ornament or sculpture: 2 rows of nodules just below the suture; coarse spiral threads.
Aperture: Small, oblique; anterior canal short. Operculum corneous, paucispiral.
Habitat: Shallow reef, sand, and algae.
Localities: Southeast.
Occurrence: Common.
Range: Southeast Florida to the West Indies; Bermuda; Brazil.
Remarks: Sometimes called Lettered Horn Shell.

Subgenus *Thericium* ('Rochebrune') Monterosato, 1890

Florida Cerith
Cerithium (Thericium) atratum
  (Born, 1778)

Size: 37 mm.
Color: White with narrow, spiral brown bands.
Shape: Elongate conic or turriculate with siphonal canal.
Ornament or sculpture: 11 to 13 slightly convex whorls; 2 to 3 white former varices on each whorl; several rows of beaded spiral cords on each whorl with finer granulated cords separating them; beads fairly regular, giving neat appearance.

Aperture: Oval, oblique; outer lip thickened into crenulated varix; parietal area glossy white; anterior siphonal canal short and upturned; posterior canal simple fold where lip joins body whorl.
Habitat: Littoral, on sea grasses; epifaunal.
Localities: Entire.
Occurrence: Common.
Range: North Carolina to southern half of Florida; Texas; Yucatán; northeastern and eastern Brazil.
Remarks: Syn. C. *floridanum* Mörch, 1876.

Muddy Cerith
Cerithium (Thericium) lutosum
  (Menke, 1828)

Size: 6–12 mm.
Color: Brown black or grayish white with mottlings of reddish brown; nuclear whorls whitish.
Shape: Elongate conic, turriculate.
Ornament or sculpture: 8 slightly convex whorls; sutures distinct; 7 to 8 beaded, spiral cords on body whorl interspaced with fine striations; repeated but fewer in number on remaining whorls; 1 to 2 former varices on each whorl.
Aperture: Oval; outer lip thin on edge with thickened varix behind edge; parietal area white and glossy but thin; columella short, edged in white with brief upturned siphonal canal; only slight posterior canal.

Habitat: Littoral, on algae and marine grass; in shallow bays; semi-epifaunal.
Localities: South.
Occurrence: Common.
Range: Bermuda; southern Florida; Texas; Gulf of Mexico to Quintana Roo; Costa Rica; West Indies.
Remarks: Syn. *C. variabile* (C. B. Adams, 1845); found on *Thalassia* grass and crawling along mud flats; more abundant in summer; animal black with white mottlings; eyes behind base of tentacles; secretes mucus thread to suspend itself; lays eggs in gelatinous strings.

Subfamily DIASTOMATINAE
Cossmann, 1895

Genus *Diastoma* DeShayes, 1850
Variable Bittium
Diastoma varium (Pfeiffer, 1840)

Size: 5–6 mm.
Color: Grayish brown.
Shape: Elongate conic, turriculate.
Ornament or sculpture: 7 to 8 slightly convex whorls, sutures definite; numerous rounded, curved transverse ribs crossed by spiral grooves that give nodulose appearance to sculpture; base has spiral grooves but not ribs.
Aperture: Oval, thin with varix adjacent; anterior siphonal canal poorly developed.
Habitat: On marine grass; in bays; epifaunal.

Localities: Entire.
Occurrence: Common.
Range: Maryland to Florida; Texas to Gulf of Campeche; Yucatán, Quintana Roo; Costa Rica; West Indies; Brazil.
Remarks: During warm months collected in vast numbers from blades of marine grass; eggs tiny, deposited in gelatinous string coiled into counterclockwise spiral; larvae planktrophic; food for drum; [*Bittium varium* Pfeiffer, 1840].

Genus *Alabina* Dall, 1902
Miniature Horn Shell
Alabina cerithidioides (Dall, 1889)

Size: 2–4 mm.
Color: Cream to light brown.
Shape: Elongate conic.
Ornament or sculpture: 8 to 10 whorls, first 3 smooth; remaining whorls with narrow, curved axial ribs and faint revolving threads.
Aperture: Somewhat rounded, outer lip thin; columella weakly curved and ending in slight lip below, behind which is small narrow umbilicus.
Habitat: Inlet areas; epifaunal.
Localities: Entire.
Occurrence: Common in beach drift.
Range: Florida; Texas; Campeche Bank; Quintana Roo; West Indies.
Remarks: Difficult to separate from *Diastoma varium* and juvenile *Cerithium lutosum*; [*Finella cerithidioides*]; *Finella dubia* (Orbigny, 1842) may be syn.

Superfamily CERITHIOPSIODEA
Family CERITHIOPSIDAE H. & A.
Adams, 1854

Genus *Cerithiopsis* Forbes & Hanley, 1849
Green's Miniature Cerith
Cerithiopsis greeni (C. B. Adams, 1839)

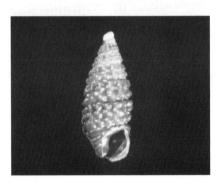

Genus *Eumetula* Thiele, 1912
Awl Miniature Cerith
Eumetula emersoni (C. B. Adams, 1838)

Size: 3 mm.
Color: Glossy brown.
Shape: Elongate conic, turriculate.
Ornament or sculpture: 9 to 12 convex whorls; nuclear whorls smooth; remaining whorls with 3 rows of glassy beads joined by spiral and transverse threads.
Aperture: Oval, lip thin; columella arched in juveniles but straight with slight, flaring anterior notch in adults.
Habitat: Bays, inlets, shelly sand; epifaunal.
Localities: entire.
Occurrence: Common.
Range: Bermuda; Cape Cod to both sides of Florida and Texas; Gulf of Mexico to Quintana Roo; Costa Rica.
Remarks: Lives on marine plants; confused with *Diastoma* but whorls are more convex and siphonal canal better developed.

Size: 12–18 mm.
Color: Light brown with suture sometimes darker.
Shape: Slender, elongate conic, awl-shaped.
Ornament or sculpture: 10 to 14 flatsided whorls, sutures distinct; 3 strong spiral rows of raised, roundish beads, revolving thread between beaded rows; faint axial ribs may connect beads; middle row of beads less prominent than others; base concave with cordlike spiral ridges and fine transverse growth lines.
Aperture: Oval; lip thin; short, slightly flared anterior siphonal canal.
Habitat: Inlet, shelly sand along shore; epifaunal.
Localities: Entire.
Occurrence: Common.
Range: Massachusetts to West Indies; Texas; Costa Rica.
Remarks: [*Cerithiopsis emersonii*]. Syn. *C. subulata* (Montagu, 1808). Looks like elongated *C. greeni* at first glance. Offshore.

Genus *Seila* A. Adams, 1861
Adams' Miniature Cerith
Seila adamsi (H. C. Lea, 1845)

Genus *Alaba* H. & A. Adams, 1853
Uncertain Miniature Cerith
Alaba incerta (Orbigny, 1842)

Size: 10 mm.
Color: Brown.
Shape: Elongate conic, nearly cylindrical.
Ornament or sculpture: About 12 flatsided whorls, regularly increasing in size; 3 strong, flattened spiral ridges on each whorl; concave spaces between them marked with fine spiral striations and delicate transverse lines that do not cross ridges; base of shell concave.
Aperture: Oval; outer lip crenulated to correspond with external sculpture; columella short, ending in centrally located siphonal canal, slightly recurved.
Habitat: Under old shell in hypersaline bays and inlets; epifaunal.
Localities: Entire.
Occurrence: Common.
Range: Bermuda; Massachusetts to Florida; Texas; Carmen, Campeche, Mexico; Gulf of Campeche; Campeche Bank; Yucatán; Costa Rica; West Indies; Brazil.
Remarks: Found by turning broken shell and examining attached algae; chalky and bleached when dead.

Size: 6 mm.
Color: Nucleus glossy brown; remainder whitish with light brown spots; translucent.
Shape: Elongate conic, slender.
Ornament or sculpture: About 13 rounded whorls, gradually increasing in size; shell thin and smooth except for numerous very fine spiral striations; raised former varices characteristic on whorls.
Aperture: Oval; lip barely thickened, smooth inside; siphonal canal not well developed.
Habitat: Among rocks in inlets and offshore on algal growths; favors *Sargassum;* epifaunal.
Localities: Southeast.
Occurrence: Fairly common in beach drift.
Range: Bermuda; southeastern Florida to Lesser Antilles and Central America; Texas; Yucatán; Quintana Roo; Bahamas; Brazil.
Remarks: Syn. *Rissoa teravaricosa* C. B. Adams, 1895.

Subfamily LITIOPINAE
H. & A. Adams, 1854

Genus *Litiopa* Rang, 1829
Brown Sargassum Snail
Litiopa melanostoma Rang, 1829

Family TRIPHORIDAE Gray, 1847

Genus *Triphora* Blainville, 1828
Black-Lined Triphora
Triphora **cf.** *perversa nigrocinta* (C. B.
Adams, 1839)

Size: 12–18 mm.
Color: Dark brown, translucent.
Shape: Moderately elongate conic.
Ornament or sculpture: 7 whorls; body whorl expanded and about half length of shell; appears smooth but covered with numerous microscopic spiral lines more strongly incised on base; nuclear whorls have regularly spaced, vertical striations.
Aperture: Semilunar with slightly convex columella; strong ridge on inside edge of columella characteristic.
Habitat: Pelagic with *Sargassum nutans* Orbigny; epifaunal.
Localities: Entire.
Occurrence: Common in beach drift.
Range: Same as *Sargassum*, including Yucatán and Quintana Roo; both sides of Panama.
Remarks: Looks very much like berry on *Sargassum*; found by shaking *Sargassum* or by sifting beach drift.

Size: 5–10 mm.
Color: Dark brown.
Shape: Elongate conic, somewhat cylindrical.
Ornament or sculpture: 10 to 12 slightly convex whorls tapering to acute apex; sutures slightly excavated; 3 spiral rows of rather evenly spaced, glossy beads that appear lighter under lens; keeled base has strong revolving cords.
Aperture: Oval, oblique, brown with thin, crenulated outer lip; well-developed posterior notch and short recurved anterior canal, in adults both become tubular; sinistral.
Habitat: High-salinity reefs on algae; epifaunal.
Localities: Entire.
Occurrence: Fairly common in beach drift.
Range: Massachusetts to Florida; Texas; Carmen, Campeche, Mexico; Gulf of Campeche; Yucatán; West Indies; Brazil.
Remarks: Easily confused with *Cerithiopsis greeni*, but "left-handed" aperture sets it apart.

Superfamily EPITONIACEA s.s. Berry, 1910
Family EPITONIIDAE s.s. Berry, 1910

Genus *Amaea* H. & A. Adams, 1854
Subgenus *Amaea* s.s.

Mitchell's Wentletrap
Amaea (Amaea) mitchelli (Dall, 1896)

Genus *Epitonium* Röding, 1798
Subgenus *Epitonium* s.s.

White Wentletrap
Epitonium (Epitonium) albidum (Orbigny, 1842)

Size: 25.6–51 mm.
Color: Pale ivory with dark brownish band at periphery and solid brownish area below basal ridge.
Shape: Elongate conic, turriculate.
Ornament or sculpture: 15 strongly convex whorls gradually increasing in size from apex to base; 22 irregular, low costae per whorl; spiral sculpture of fine threads produces definite reticulated pattern; thickened ridge and brownish color define basal area.
Aperture: Subcircular; thickened, nonreflected lip; columella short, arched.
Habitat: Offshore; epifaunal.
Localities: West.
Occurrence: Uncommon.
Range: Western Florida; Texas to Yucatan; Caribbean coast of Panama; Surinam.
Remarks: Until R/V *Pillsbury* expedition to Gulf of Panama in 1967, thought to be indigenous to Texas; holotype collected ca. 1894 on Matagorda Island, Texas, by J. D. Mitchell.

Size: 20 mm.
Color: Shiny white.
Shape: Elongate conic, turriculate.
Ornament or sculpture: 9 to 11 gradually increasing, moderately convex whorls, attached by costae only; bladelike transverse costae rather low and generally fused with costae on previous whorl; body whorl contains 12 to 14 unangled costae; may have microscopic spiral threads but not strong enough to be grouped with those considered to have spiral striations; anomphalous.
Aperture: Subcircular; outer lip expanded, reflected; parietal area narrow, slightly thickened, held away from body whorl by costae; nearly holostomatous.
Habitat: Intertidal to 360 meters (200 fathoms); epifaunal.
Localities: Entire.
Occurrence: Fairly common in beach drift.
Range: Bermuda; Florida; Texas; Costa Rica; West Indies; Surinam; south to northern Argentina; west Africa.
Remarks: Low ribs appear to form continuous oblique lines bottom to top.

Angulate Wentletrap
Epitonium (Epitonium) angulatum
  (Say, 1831)

Humphrey's Wentletrap
Epitonium (Epitonium) cf. *E. humphreysi*
  (Kiener, 1838)

Size: 19–25 mm.
Color: Glossy white.
Shape: Elongate conic, turriculate.
Ornament or sculpture: 8 moderately convex whorls gradually increasing in size from apex; sculpture on whorls of numerous reflected, bladelike costae; costae form angles on shoulder of each whorl, stronger on early whorls, a little less to almost absent on later whorls; costae in line with those on whorl above and fused where they meet; anomphalous.
Aperture: Subcircular; outer lip thickened, held away from body whorls by costae; columella not defined.
Habitat: Intertidal to moderate depths with sea anemones; epifaunal.
Localities: Entire.
Occurrence: Common in beach drift.
Range: Bermuda; eastern end of Long Island to Florida (excluding lower Keys); Texas; Brazil.
Remarks: Some specimens more slender than typical form and can be confused with *E. humphreysi* (Kiener); juvenile shell more strongly angulated than adult; as shell reaches maturity, costae become more thickened and rounded.

Size: 12–20 mm.
Color: Flat white.
Shape: Elongate conic, turriculate.
Ornament or sculpture: 9 to 10 strongly convex whorls; numerous bladelike to rounded costae on whorls, also serve to connect whorls; suture deep; costae more bladelike on early whorls, becoming thickened and rounded with maturity; may be reflected and angled at whorl shoulder, especially on early whorls; body whorl has 8 to 9 costae; anomphalous.
Aperture: Subcircular; outer lip expanded; usually thickened; parietal lip thin, tightly pressed to body whorl; columella short, arched.
Habitat: Inlet areas and along shore on sandy bottoms; epifaunal.
Localities: Entire.
Occurrence: Fairly common in beach drift.
Range: Cape Cod south to Florida (not lower Keys) and west to Texas; Carmen, Campeche, Mexico.
Remarks: Difficult to distinguish from *E. angulatum* (Say); if typical, more narrow, costae more rounded, less developed shoulder angle but very variable.

Tollin's Wentletrap
Epitonium (Epitonium) cf. *E tollini*
  Bartsch, 1938

Subgenus *Gyroscala* Boury, 1887

Brown-Banded Wentletrap
Epitonium (Gyroscala) rupicola (Kurtz, 1860)

Size: 14 mm.
Color: White.
Shape: Elongate conic, turriculate.
Ornament or sculpture: 9 to 10 convex whorls that can be adpressed or separated and attached by costae only; numerous bladelike costae, 11 to 16 on body whorl; costae spaced irregularly, not always lined up with those on whorl above; even in height throughout with occasional thick one, especially on body whorl; not angled at shoulder, and no spiral sculpture; suture deep; anomphalous.
Aperture: Subcircular; outer lip thickened, reflected; parietal area thin, pressed closely to body wall; columella short, arched.
Habitat: Probably intertidal; epifaunal.
Localities: West.
Occurrence: Common in beach drift.
Range: Western Floria from Marco Island north to Gasparilla Island; Texas.
Remarks: Look for mismatched costae and occasional large one.

Size: 12–20 mm.
Color: White to cream with 2 brownish, spiral bands at suture; costae white.
Shape: Elongate conic, turriculate.
Ornament or sculpture: 11 globose whorls attached at sutures; suture deep; transverse sculpture consists of numerous low, bladelike costae, interspersed with rounded varices; height and number of costae variable, not lined up with costae on adjoining whorl; basal ridge well defined with thin, threadlike line.
Aperture: Subcircular; lip slightly thickened, reflected; nearly entire.
Habitat: Below low water to 36 meters (20 fathoms); epifaunal.
Localities: Entire.
Occurrence: Fairly common in beach drift.
Range: Massachusetts south to Florida and west to Texas; Surinam.
Remarks: Look for brown bands.

Subgenus *Asperiscala* Boury, 1909

Dall's Wentletrap
Epitonium (Asperiscala) cf. *E. apiculatum*
(Dall, 1889)

Multiribbed Wentletrap
Epitonium (Asperiscala) multistriatum
(Say, 1826)

Size: 4.5 mm.
Color: White.
Shape: Elongate conic, turriculate.
Ornament or sculpture: 9 convex whorls attached by costae only; axial sculpture consists of numerous bladelike costae; 11 costae on body whorl; nuclear whorls smooth; first 3 postnuclear whorls possess costae which are low, cordlike, and far more numerous than those on remaining whorls; spiral, threadlike cord only on first 3 postnuclear whorls; later whorls have strong bladelike costae.
Aperture: Circular with thickened, expanded lip; umbilical area partially closed by parietal thickening; columella short, arched.
Habitat: Probably along shore; epifaunal.
Localities: Entire.
Occurrence: Uncommon in beach drift.
Range: South Carolina; Texas; Puerto Rico.
Remarks: Could be aberrant form of some other species, which may explain limited distribution.

Size: 15 mm.
Color: White.
Shape: Elongate conic, turriculate.
Ornament or sculpture: 8 to 10 strongly convex whorls, later ones unattached; suture deep; transverse sculpture consists of very numerous cordlike to low bladelike costae not angled at shoulder; many finely incised lines between these that do not cross ribs; apical whorls much smaller in proportion to later ones and have more ribs; anomphalous.
Aperture: More oval than round with very narrowly expanded lip; columella not defined; parietal lip tightly pressed to parietal area.
Habitat: Offshore, epifaunal.
Localities: West.
Occurrence: Uncommon.
Range: Bermuda; Massachusetts south to Cape Canaveral and west to Texas; Brazil.
Remarks: Many ribs and more delicate appearance than other *Epitonium* make identification easy.

New England Wentletrap
Epitonium (Asperiscala) novangliae
(Courthouy, 1838)

Subgenus *Depressicala* Boury, 1909
Epitonium (Depressicala) nautlae
(Mörch, 1874)

Family JANTHINADAE Leach, 1823

Genus *Janthina* Röding, 1798
Subgenus *Jodina* Mörch, 1860

Dwarf Purple Sea Snail
Janthina (Jodina) globosa Blainville, 1822

Size: 14 mm.
Color: White, banded with light brown above and below periphery of whorl; often light brown throughout.
Shape: Elongate conic, turriculate.
Ornament or sculpture: 8 to 10 strongly convex whorls gradually increasing in size from apex, later whorls attached by costae only; numerous bladelike to cordlike costae, latter as a result of costae being reflected back and down; body whorl has 9 to 16 costae angled or hooked at shoulder; spiral sculpture reticulated pattern formed by numerous spiral threads crossed by finer transverse lines; no basal ridge.
Aperture: Subcircular with narrow expanded lip; parietal lip only moderately thickened, pressed to body whorl above umbilicus.
Habitat: Offshore; epifaunal.
Localities: Entire.
Occurrence: Fairly common.
Range: Bermuda; Massachusetts; Virginia south to Campeche Bank; Brazil.
Remarks: Although called New England Wentletrap, it does not live north of Virginia.

Size: 6–19 mm.
Color: Deep violet.
Shape: Globose ovate.
Ornament or sculpture: Thin shell faintly striated, with striae following edge of aperture; at indentation of latter they curve, forming distinct keel on last whorl.
Aperture: Outer lip deeply indented at midwhorl point.
Habitat: Pelagic.
Localities: Entire.
Occurrence: Common.
Range: Worldwide.
Remarks: Float comparatively small; egg cases of this hermaphrodite pear-shaped and contain about 75 eggs; syn. *J. umblicata* Orbigny, 1940; "*J. exigua* Lamarck*" of authors, not Lamarck, 1816.

Subgenus *Janthina* s.s.
Common Purple Sea Snail
Janthina (Janthina) janthina (Linné, 1758)

Pale Purple Sea Snail
Janthina (Janthina) pallida
(Thompson, 1841)

Size: 32 mm.
Color: Purple on basal part of shell, lavender or white above (floats with purple side up).
Shape: Low conic; body whorl very large and gently angular.
Ornament or sculpture: Smooth, very fragile.
Aperture: More or less subquadrate with columellar edge almost vertical; outer lip very delicate, lower edge horizontal.
Habitat: Pelagic in warm seas.
Localities: Entire.
Occurrence: Seasonally common.
Range: Pelagic in most warm seas.
Remarks: Foot builds float by trapping air bubbles in mucus; exudes purple stain when disturbed; carnivorous, feeding on Portuguese men-of-war, *Velella,* and other violet-colored coelenterates; strong southeast wind in spring will literally cover beach with them, next year might not appear at all; beware of Portuguese men-of-war that wash in with them.

Size: 12–18 mm.
Color: Purplish white with pale lavender on early whorls and along margin of outer lip.
Shape: Globose conic.
Ornament or sculpture: Appears smooth but has fine, irregular axial growth lines; body whorl large, rounded, swollen.
Aperture: Subquadrate, somewhat flaring at base; thin outer margin of lip slightly sinuate near center where float attached; interior violet along columella and base, fainter over remainder.
Habitat: Pelagic in warm seas.
Localities: Entire.
Occurrence: Uncommon, seasonal.
Range: Pelagic in most warm seas.
Remarks: Easily confused with *J. prolongata,* only recently recognized as occurring in this area; attaches eggs to bottom of float.

Subgenus *Violetta* Iredale, 1929

Globe Purple Sea Snail
Janthina (Violetta) prolongata
  Blainville, 1822

Size: 12–18 mm.
Color: Deep violet throughout.
Shape: Globose with low spire; body whorl
very large.
Ornament or sculpture: Smooth, very
fragile; very fine growth lines.
Aperture: Subquadrate, very large;
columella vertical; outer lip has sinuous
margin; indentation marks point of
attachment of float.
Habitat: Pelagic in warm seas.
Localities: Entire.
Occurrence: Fairly common.
Range: Pelagic in warm waters; both coasts
of United States.
Remarks: Syn. *J. globosa* (Swainson, 1823)
[not Blainville, 1822]; attaches eggs to float;
less numerous and more delicate than *J.
janthina*; remove animals by "watering out"
(see Cleaning).

Genus *Recluzia* Petit de la Saussaye, 1853

Brown Sea Snail
Recluzia rollaniana Petit, 1853 [See *SST*,
  p. 115]

Superfamily EULIMACEA Risso, 1826
Family EULIMIDAE Risso, 1826

Genus *Niso* Risso, 1826
Niso aegless Bush, 1885 [See *SST*, p. 116]

Genus *Eulima* Risso, 1826 =
  [*Strombiformis* of authors, not Da
  Costa, 1778]

Two-Lined Melanella
Eulima cf. *E. bilineatus* (Alder, 1848)

Size: 8 mm.
Color: Whitish with 2 brownish lines on
each whorl; polished.
Shape: Elongate conic, very slender.
Ornament or sculpture: 10 flattened
whorls, sutures fairly distinct; gradually
tapers to sharp apex that may be deflected.
Aperture: Elongated pyriform; entire; outer
lip sharp; columella concave.
Habitat: Thought to be ectoparasitic on
holothurians in shallow waters; epifaunal.
Localities: Entire.
Occurrence: Fairly common.
Range: Europe; North Carolina to West
Indies; Texas; Brazil.
Remarks: [*Strombiformis bilineata*]. Syn. *S.
bifaciatus*.

Genus Melanella Bowdich, 1822

Curved Melanella
Melanella arcuanta C. B. Adams, 1850

Genus *Polygireulima* Sacco, 1892

Jamaica Melanella
Polygireulima jamaicensis (C. B. Adams, 1845)

Size: 4 mm.
Color: Glossy white.
Shape: Ovate conic.
Ornament or sculpture: 10 convex whorls with lightly impressed suture; fine impressed spiral line above suture marks smooth shell; spire with axis curved to extraordinary degree in upper whorls.
Aperture: Rather long ovate.
Habitat: Ectoparasitic on sea cucumbers; epifaunal.
Localities: Entire.
Occurrence: Fairly common.
Range: North Carolina; Texas; West Indies.
Remarks: Type specimen lost. [*Balcis arcuata*].

Size: 6–12 mm.
Color: Glossy white.
Shape: Elongate conic.
Ornament or sculpture: 12 to 14 flat-sided whorls; polished whorls taper to slightly bent sharp apex; sutures not well defined; anomphalous.
Aperture: Pyriform, slender; outer lip thin but slightly thickened at base; columella concave.
Habitat: Ectoparasitic; bays; epifaunal.
Localities: Entire.
Occurrence: Common.
Range: Florida; Texas; Carmen, Campeche, Mexico; Gulf of Campeche; Costa Rica[?]; West Indies.
Remarks: May be *Melanella intermedia* Contraine, 1835; has been referred to as *Balcis conoidea* Kurtz & Stimpson, 1851, but lacks distinct basal ridge and rhomboidal aperture of that species. Syn. *P. intermedia* Contraine. [*Balcis jamaicensis* C. B. Adams]

Superfamily STROMBACEA
Rafinesque, 1815
Family STROMBIDAE Rafinesque, 1815

Genus *Strombus* Linné, 1758
Fighting Conch
Strombus alatus Gmelin, 1791

ribbons. Look for it on sandbars as the tide
starts to come in.

Hawk-Wing Conch
Strombus rainus Gmelin, 1791

Size: 75–100 mm.
Color: Dark reddish brown to lighter
brown; some mottled or with zigzag
markings.
Shape: Conic.
Ornament or sculpture: Spire has 8 whorls;
body whorl is four-fifths of total length of
heavy, solid shell; wide shoulders with or
without short spines; spiral striations near
base; sutures distinct; anomphalous.
Aperture: Long narrow; lip has broad
outward flare; interior polished; somewhat
flared siphonal notch at base and rounded
notch in lip just above it.
Habitat: Intertidal to about 18 meters (10
fathoms); epifaunal.
Localities: Entire.
Occurrence: Common.
Range: South Carolina; both sides of
Florida; Texas.
Remarks: This grazing scavenger has well-
developed eyes on long eye stalks on head;
long, narrow foot tipped with clawlike
operculum moves animal about in awkward
leaps; can right itself and return to water if
beached by wave; eggs laid in gelatinous

Size: 9 cm.
Color: Grayish with brown mottling.
Shape: Conical body with winglike
extension of outerlip.
Ornament or sculpture: Bluntly spinose,
largest spines are the last 2 on body whorl.
Aperture: Heavy folds in upper parietal
corner. Salmon pink inside. Interior and lip
glazed. Operculum small, corneous,
clawlike.
Habitat: Sandy bottoms.
Localities: Southeast; Keys.
Occurrence: Common to uncommon.
Range: Southeast Florida to the West
Indies; Bermuda; Brazil.
Remarks: Syn. *S. bituberculatus* Lamarck,
1822. Common on sandbars in Keys and
West Indies. Do not collect during
March–April mating season.

Superfamily CALYPTRAEACEA
Blainville, 1824
Family CALYPTRAEIDAE Blainville, 1824

Genus *Crucibulum* Schumacher, 1817

West Indian Cup and Saucer
Crucibulum auricula (Gmelin, 1791)

Subfamily CREPIDULINAE Fleming, 1822

Genus *Crepidula* Lamarck, 1799
Subgenus *Crepidula* s.s.

Faded Slipper Shell
Crepidula (Crepidula) convexa Say, 1822

Size: 2.5 cm. diameter.
Color: Grayish, interior pinkish.
Shape: Cap-shaped with a cuplike support.
Ornament or sculpture: Coarse diagonal exterior ribs and crenelated edges.
Aperture: Wide, edges of inner cup are completely free. No operculum.
Habitat: On other shells.
Localities: West.
Occurrence: Uncommon.
Range: West Florida to the West Indies; Brazil.
Remarks: Originally *Patella auricula* Gmelin 1791.

Size: Length 12 mm, width 8 mm.
Color: Translucent tan or mottled with reddish brown; internal septum white.
Shape: Limpetlike, low, oval with apex near margin; varies corresponding to shape of attachment site.
Ornament or sculpture: Smooth with centrally located apex.
Aperture: Very large oval with thin margin; internal deck, or septum, deep-seated, convex, supports soft parts.
Habitat: Intertidal to moderate depths on shell, rocks, grass; epifaunal.
Localities: Entire.
Occurrence: Common.
Range: Bermuda; Massachusetts to Florida; Texas; Yucatán; Quintana Roo; West Indies; California.
Remarks: Commensal with living *Argopecten irradians amplicostatus* and some gastropods, preferring to be near outer lip of host.

Common Atlantic Slipper Shell
Crepidula (Crepidula) fornicata (Linné, 1758)

Spotted Slipper Shell
Crepidula maculosa (Conrad, 1869)

Size: 51 mm.
Color: Dirty white to tan with mottlings of brown shades.
Shape: Limpetlike, oval oblique; curved to fit place of attachment.
Ornament or sculpture: Smooth except for fine growth lines; body whorl major part of shell; apex turned to one side.
Aperture: Oval, oblique, with thin margin; polished interior; deck occupies about half of aperture; white margin sinuous.
Habitat: 1 to 8 meters (6 fathoms); epifaunal on exoskeleton.
Localities: Entire.
Occurrence: Common.
Range: Canada to Florida and Texas; Yucatán; introduced to California and England.
Remarks: Adult shell sedentary and tends to pile up in stacks of up to 19 individuals that gradually diminish in size; frequently on olive shells; stack of protandric mollusks will have right margin of each member in contact with right margin of one it is on; bottom and larger animals are female, top are males, and those in between are in transitional stages; eggs brooded in mantle cavity.

Size: 3.1 cm. × 2.5 cm.
Color: Whitish, irregularly spotted with purple-brown blotches or streaks.
Shape: Oval, limpetlike; shelly platform has straight edge.
Ornament or sculpture: Smooth with faint growth lines.
Aperture: Wide, oval, single muscle scar visible on white interior. No operculum.
Habitat: On rock and old shell in shallow water.
Localities: Entire.
Occurrence: Fairly common.
Range: Florida; Mexico; Bahamas.
Remarks: Formerly considered to be *C. fornicata.*

Subgenus *Ianacus* Mörch, 1852

Eastern White Slipper Shell
Crepidula (Ianacus) plana Say, 1822

Superfamily TRIVIACEA Gray, 1852
Family TRIVIIDAE Gray, 1852
Subfamily TRIVIINAE Troschel, 1863

Genus *Trivia* Gray, 1852
Subgenus *Pusula* Jousseaume, 1884

Suffuse Trivia
Trivia (Pusula) suffusa (Gray, 1832) [See *SST*, p. 122]

Superfamily CYPRAEACEA Rafinesque, 1815
Family CYPRAEIDAE Rafinesque, 1815
Subfamily CYPRAEINAE Rafinesque, 1815

Genus *Cypraea* Linné, 1758
Subgenus *Macrocypraea* Schilder, 1930

Atlantic Deer Cowrie
Cypraea (Macrocypraea) cervus Linné, 1771

Size: Length up to 30 mm.
Color: White.
Shape: Elongate oval, flat; conforms to attachment site.
Ornament or sculpture: Smooth except for fine growth lines; apex depressed.
Aperture: Large, oval with thin margin; deck about half length of shell, notched to one side; polished.
Habitat: Intertidal to moderate depths; epifaunal.
Localities: Entire.
Occurrence: Common.
Range: Bermuda; Canada to Florida; Gulf states; Texas; Gulf of Mexico to Quintana Roo; rare in West Indies; Surinam; Brazil.
Remarks: Not as particular as to attachment site as *C. fornicata* and *C. convexa*—dead shell, old bottles, piers, oysters, tires, all will do; as a result shape of this flat shell can be quite varied; eggs brooded under shell.

Family OVULIDAE Gray, 1853

Genus *Simnialena* Cate, 1973

Single-Toothed Simnia
Simnialena uniplicata (G. B. Sowerby
 II, 1848)

Size: 75–125 mm.
Color: Polished light brown, with large, round, white spots on dorsal side; whitish dorsal line.
Shape: Elongate oval; spire concealed.
Ornament or sculpture: Smooth, polished.
Aperture: Long, narrow; outer lip rolled inward, brownish without spots; edge outlined with regular, small, alternating brown and white riblets; similar but less distinct riblets on inner lip; purplish interior.
Habitat: Offshore reefs; epifaunal.
Localities: Southeast; south; Keys.
Occurrence: Common.
Range: Southeastern Florida to Yucatán; Brazil.
Remarks: Pinkish brown and whitish mantle covered with short papillae and envelops entire shell; at rest, shell is covered, but when touched, animal draws into shell; female lays eggs in gelatinous mass of 500 to 1,500 capsules, which she broods; this carnivore grazes on algae and colonial invertebrates; nocturnal; beach shells have smooth worn place on underside parallel to aperture.

Size: 20.2 mm.
Color: Deep rose brown overall, except that outer lip, front base, adaxial carina, and portions of rear terminal beak white.
Shape: Long, narrow, subcylindrical; ends tapering.
Ornament or sculpture: Smooth, glossy except for incised striae restricted to either end.
Aperture: Broad, flaring toward front; outer lip thinly, roundly thickened, with weak callus shouldering above.
Habitat: On soft coral, *Eugorgia virgulata;* epifaunal.
Localities: South; Keys.
Occurrence: Uncommon.
Range: Virginia to both coasts of Florida; possibly Honduras and east coast of Central America.
Remarks: Previously misidentified (J. Andrews 1971, p. 98) as *Neosimnia acicularis* (Lamarck, 1810), which is *Cymbula acicularis.*

Superfamily NATICACEA (Swainson),
Gray, 1840
Family NATICIDAE (Swainson),
Gray, 1840
Subfamily POLINICINAE Gray, 1847

Genus *Polinices* Montfort, 1810
Subgenus *Neverita* Risso, 1826

Shark's Eye
Polinices (Neverita) duplicatus (Say, 1822)

Aperture: Large, subcircular; outer lip thin; columella oblique; umbilicus deep, partly closed by heavy callus; no siphonal canal.
Habitat: Shallow waters of both bay and Gulf; infaunal.
Localities: Entire.
Occurrence: Common.
Range: Cape Cod to Florida and Gulf states.
Remarks: Plows through sand in search of bivalves and snails; wraps foot about prey, begins slow process of drilling round hole in shell, inserting proboscis, and rasping out soft parts with radula, often tiring before completion; does not feed unless buried; female builds collar of mucus and sand over margin of aperture when spawning. The bay form is darker, rounder, and more elevated than those offshore.

Subgenus *Polinices* s.s.

Brown Moon Shell
Polinices (Polinices) hepaticus (Röding, 1798)

Size: Diameter 26–37 mm.
Color: Porcelaneous, glossy, gray to tan, often strikingly marked with orange brown; underside whitish; callus in bay specimens often rich purple.
Shape: Globose, low spire, expanded body whorl; bay specimens have higher spires than Gulf ones.
Ornament or sculpture: Smooth with fine growth lines.

Size: 2.5–5.1 cm.
Color: Exterior purplish brown and orange brown.
Shape: Globose, elongate oval.
Ornament or sculpture: Polished, heavy. About 3 whorls. Body whorl dominates shell. Fine, irregular growth lines.
Aperture: Semilunar. Columella and interior white. Umbilicus white, large, deep. Operculum corneous, paucispiral.
Habitat: Shallow, sandy bottoms offshore. Infaunal.

Localities: Southeast; Keys.
Occurrence: Uncommon.
Range: Southeastern Florida; Texas; West Indies; Surinam; Brazil.
Remarks: Predatory carnivore. Bores holes in bivalves with radula. Deposits eggs in sand collars.

Subfamily NATICINAE Swainson, 1840

Genus *Natica* Scopoli, 1777
Subgenus *Naticarius* Dumeril, 1806
Colorful Atlantic Natica
Natica (Naticarius) canrena (Linné, 1758)

Size: 25–51 mm.
Color: White or cream with variable brown markings that may be axial zigzag marks superimposed over spiral bands alternating tan and white.
Shape: Subglobular.
Ornament or sculpture: Smooth; spire depressed; body whorl expanded. Faint waves near sutures.
Aperture: Large, semilunar. Thin outer lip. Callus large, white, entering deep umbilicus. Brownish on interior.
Habitat: Sandy bottoms beyond low tide. Infaunal.
Localities: Entire.
Occurrence: Common.
Range: Bermuda; southeastern United States to West Indies; Texas; Campeche Bank; Yucatán; Surinam; Brazil.
Remarks: Lives offshore, seldom reaches the beaches.

Subgenus *Tectonatica* Sacco, 1890
Miniature Natica
Natica (Tectonatica) pusilla Say, 1822

Size: Diameter 6–8 mm.
Color: White to fawn brown, faint reddish brown markings.
Shape: Subglobular; spire depressed, body whorl expanded.
Ornament or sculpture: Smooth with fine growth lines, porcelaneous.
Aperture: Large, semilunar; outer lip thin; columella oblique; callus strong, practically covering umbilicus, but often has small opening next to umbilical callus.
Habitat: Shallow inlet areas; infaunal.
Localities: Entire.
Occurrence: Fairly common.
Range: Eastern United States; Gulf states; Carmen, Campeche, Mexico; Gulf of Campeche; West Indies; Surinam; northeastern Brazil.
Remarks: Corneous operculum distinguishes it from similar appearance of juvenile *Polinices duplicatus.*

Subfamily SININAE Woodring, 1928

Genus *Sinum* Röding, 1798

Maculated Baby's Ear
Sinum maculatum (Say, 1831)

Common Baby's Ear
Sinum perspectivum (Say, 1831)

Size: 2.5–3.1 cm.
Color: All brown or blotched with brown.
Shape: Auriform, slightly elevate.
Ornament or sculpture: About 3 whorls.
Sutures only slightly impressed. Very weak
spiral growth lines on top of whorls.
Aperture: Large, rounded. Outer lip sharp.
Columella curved. No operculum.
Habitat: Offshore. Infaunal.
Localities: South and West.
Occurrence: Uncommon.
Range: Southeastern United States.
West Indies.
Remarks: Shell heavier and more elevated
than *S. perspectivum*.

Size: Diameter 25–51 m.
Color: White.
Shape: Auriform, greatly flattened; apex on
same plane as body whorl.
Ornament or sculpture: About 3 whorls;
sutures slightly impressed; many fine spiral
growth lines on top of whorls.
Aperture: Large, rounded; outer lip sharp;
columella curved.
Habitat: Along outer beaches and inlet
areas in sand; infaunal.
Localities: Entire.
Occurrence: Common.
Range: Bermuda; southeastern United
States; Gulf states; Campeche Bank; West
Indies; Surinam; Brazil.
Remarks: Animal almost completely
envelops shell; exudes surprising quantity of
clear mucus when touched; at low tide, fed
on by raccoons.

Superfamily TONNACEA Suter, 1913
Family CASSIDAE Latreille, 1825

Genus *Phalium* Link, 1807
Subgenus *Tylocassis* Woodring, 1928

Scotch Bonnet
Phalium (Tylocassis) granulatum
granulatum (Born, 1780)

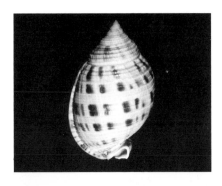

Aperture: Semilunar, length of body whorl;
outer lip thickened, reflexed with regular,
small teeth on both edges; interior fawn
colored; parietal wall glazed, smooth with
lower area pustulose; short siphonal canal
upturned to left.
Habitat: Just offshore in warm seas;
epifaunal.
Localities: Entire.
Occurrence: Fairly common.
Range: Bermuda; North Carolina to Gulf
states; West Indies; Surinam; Brazil.
Remarks: Mantle cream colored with close
dark spots; predatory on sand dollars and
sea urchins; eggs laid in tower of horny
capsules. Common offshore where it is
taken in scallop trawls.

Genus *Cassis* Scopoli, 1777

Queen Helmet
Cassis madagascariensis Lamarck, 1822

Size: Length 25–100 mm.
Color: Background white or cream with
spiral bands of regularly spaced yellowish
brown squares.
Shape: Oval with slightly extended spire.
Ornament or sculpture: Body whorl about
three-fourths of shell length; some
specimens have small nodules on shoulder
edge; deeply grooved spirally, raised spiral
cords slightly convex and wider than spaces
between them; transverse sculpture of fine
lines gives overall reticulated pattern.

Size: 10.16–15.24 cm.
Color: Light cream; parietal wall and outer
lip pale to deep salmon; teeth white with
brown between them.
Shape: Fusiform, solid.

Ornament or sculpture: Three spiral rows of blunt spines.
Aperture: Parietal shield and outer lip are pale to deep salmon. Operculum chitinous, elongate-oval.
Habitat: 3 to 10 fathoms.
Localities: Southeast.
Occurrence: Fairly common.
Range: North Carolina; Florida; West Indies; Bermuda.
Remarks: Becoming rare in Florida as a result of being caught in large numbers by scallop trawlers. Carnivorous, feeds on sea urchins. Sometimes called Emperor's Helmet.

Genus *Cypraecassis* Stutchbury, 1837

Reticulated Cowerie-Helmet
Cypraecassis testiculus Linné, 1758

Early whorls spirally grooved, body whorl reticulated. Suture slightly indented.
Aperture: Parietal shield and outer lip are pale to deep salmon. Operculum absent in adults.
Habitat: Reef inhabitant, sandy and rocky bottom, offshore.
Localities: Southeast; Keys.
Occurrence: Uncommon.
Range: North Carolina; Florida; West Indies; Bermuda; Brazil.
Remarks: Originally *Buccinum testiculus* (Linné, 1758).

Family TONNIDAE Suter, 1913

Genus *Tonna* Brunnich, 1772

Giant Tun Shell
Tonna galea (Linné, 1758)

(juvenile)

Size: 2.5–7.62 cm.
Color: Pale orange-brown with white and purplish-brown blotches.
Shape: Fusiform, with low spire.
Ornament or sculpture: 7 to 8 rather solid whorls. Body whorl almost entire length.

Size: Up to 160 mm.
Color: Creamy white to light coffee brown, generally uniform.
Shape: Globose; spire slightly extended, thin.
Ornament or sculpture: 7 to 7½ very convex whorls; body whorl dominates shell; suture deep, channeled; spiral sculpture consists of 19 to 21 rather broad, flattened ridges; usually finer ridge between 2 or larger ones on upper half of whorl; fine axial growth lines; umbilicate.
Aperture: Subovate, large; outer lip thin, crenulate until maturity; at maturity becomes reflexed and develops thickened ridge well below lip margin; parietal area glazed; columella short, twisted with ridge along outer edge that ends at siphonal canal.
Habitat: Near-shore sandy bottoms and inlet areas; epifaunal.
Localities: Entire.
Occurrence: Common offshore.
Range: North Carolina to Florida; Gulf states; Campeche Bank; West Indies; Surinam; Brazil; Indo-Pacific; Mediterranean.
Remarks: Free-swimming, pelagic young may be found in spring in beach drift; embryonic shells smooth, golden brown in color, and somewhat pliable; 3 to 4 whorls; aperture closed with tightly fitting operculum; in winter months on upper Mexican Gulf beaches, drift may be lined with young tuns about size of egg; animal has large foot and long proboscis, is yellowish in color and heavily mottled with black.

Family FICIDAE Conrad, 1867

Genus *Ficus* Röding, 1798

Common Fig Shell
Ficus communis (Röding, 1798)

Size: 7.62 cm.
Color: Cream with faint yellow-brown dots.
Shape: Turnip-shaped; thin-shelled, no spire.
Ornament or sculpture: 4 whorls, surfaced with fine growth lines crossed by spiral, cordlike ribs.
Aperture: Large, lip thin and sharp. No operculum.
Habitat: Shallow water; sand.
Localities: Entire.
Occurrence: Uncommon.
Range: North Carolina; Florida to Gulf of Mexico.
Remarks: *Syn. Pyrula communis.* Exposed at low tide.

Superfamily CYMATIACEA ?Iredale, 1913
Family CYMATIIDAE Iredale, 1913

Genus *Cymatium* Röding, 1798

Angular Triton
Cymatium femorale (Linné, 1758)

Subgenus *Gutturnium* Mörch, 1852

Knobbed Triton
Cymatium (Gutturnium) muricinum
(Röding, 1798)

Size: 10.16–17.78 cm.
Color: Orange to brown with white
nodules on the varices of last 2 to 3 whorls.
Shape: Triangular.
Ornament or sculpture: Outer lip
thickened, flaring with 6 to 8 nodules.
Aperture: Obliquely oval, siphonal canal
elongated and recurved.
Habitat: Shallow water; eel-grass, sandy
bottoms.
Localities: Southeast; Keys.
Occurrence: Uncommon to rare.
Range: Southeast Florida; West Indies;
Bermuda; Brazil.
Remarks: Syn *C. lotorium* (Lamarck, 1816).
Originally *Murex femorale* Linné, 1758.
Animal is reddish brown with dark brown
spots. Once moderately common.

Size: 2.5–7.5 cm.
Color: Gray to brown with reddish-brown
spiral bands or last whorl; white underside.
Shape: Conic with extended siphonal
canal.
Ornament or sculpture: 5 to 7 post-
embryonic convex whorls. Sutures irregular,
slightly indented. Spiral sculpture consists
of numerous nodulose cords of unequal
strength with finer threadlike striations.
Transverse sculpture of 7–8 knobbed
varices with 2–3 nodulose ridges in
between giving shell rough appearance.
Aperture: Oval with greatly thickened outer
lip. Parietal area forms large shield. Both
areas glazed white. Outer lip has 7 strong
teeth. Operculum corneous, unguiculate;
nucleus apical; numerous concentric
growth rings.
Habitat: Intertidal reefs in warm seas.
Epifaunal.
Localities: Southeast; Keys.
Occurrence: Uncommon.
Range: Southeast Florida to Brazil;
Bermuda; Texas; Indo-Pacific.

Remarks: Predatory on other mollusks and starfish.

Subgenus Cymatriton Clench & Turner, 1957

Gold-Mouthed Triton
Cymatium (Cymatriton) nicobaricum
(Röding, 1798)

oval; subcentral nucleus with concentric growth lines.
Habitat: Offshore. Epifaunal.
Localities: South; Keys.
Occurrence: Fairly common.
Range: Southeastern Florida to Brazil; Texas; Campeche Bank; Yucatán; Indo-Pacific.
Remarks: Predatory on other mollusks and starfish. [*C. chlorostomum* Lamarck, 1822].

Subgenus *Septa* Perry, 1810

Atlantic Hairy Triton
Cymatium (Septa) pileare (Linné, 1758)

Size: 3.1–5.1 cm.
Color: White or gray, mottled with reddish brown. Reddish brown spiral threads.
Shape: Conic ovate with siphonal canal; spire extended at 45° angle.
Ornament or sculpture: About 7 whorls, strongly convex; 6 strong spiral cords. Noduled cords interspaced with fine threadlike cords. 5–8 transverse varices with 3–5 knobs between each pair of varices. Anomphalous.
Aperture: Obliquely oval. Bright orange with 7 single, large white teeth on inside of outer lip. Outer lip thickened, crenulated. Teeth extend into aperture, may be single or divided. Parietal lip narrow with numerous low lamellae. Columella curved convexly. Short siphonal canal usually upturned. Operculum broadly

Size: Up to 13.1 cm.
Color: Grayish brown to golden brown, banded with alternating light and dark bands.
Shape: Elongate conic with extended siphonal canal.
Ornament or sculpture: 7–8 whorls, shoulder of body whorl about midway. Suture slightly indented. Numerous, unequal, nodulose spiral cords and fine transverse lines; 3–5 knobbed varices.
Aperture: Elliptical. Reddish-brown outer lip with 12–14 whitish plicae thickened into varix. Parietal area dark chocolate brown,

with numerous fine, irregular, white lamellae. Columella convex. Siphonal canal short, upturned. Operculun brown, corneous, unguiculate; nucleus marginal.
Habitat: Offshore to 411 meters.
Localities: Southeast.
Occurrence: Fairly common.
Range: North Carolina, Florida to West Indies; Texas; Mexico; Venezuela; Surinam; Brazil.
Remarks: This is one for divers. A long veliger stage permits wide distribution. Embryonic shell is very different from the adult. Predatory and bisexual. Syn. *C. martinianum* Orbigny, 1845.

Subgenus *Linatella* Gray, 1857

Poulsen's Triton
Cymatium (Linatella) cingulatum
(Lamarck, 1822)

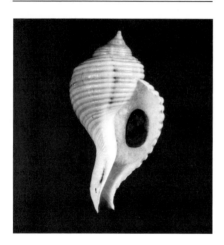

Size: 31–62 mm.
Color: Light brown to straw yellow, occasionally banded with brown.
Shape: Globose conic with extended siphonal canal.
Ornament or sculpture: 4 post-embryonic whorls; convex; body whorl slightly shouldered; suture slightly indented; spiral sculpture consists of 18 to 20 flattened cords with fine threads in between; shoulder cord might be slightly beaded; transverse sculpture of fine growth lines;

some with thin, bladelike varix; anomphalous.
Aperture: Subelliptical; outer lip crenulated, slightly expanded; parietal area glazed; columella arched inward, continuing as margin of siphonal canal; canal variable, moderately long, upturned.
Habitat: Offshore to 411 meteres (209 fathoms); epifaunal.
Localities: Entire.
Occurrence: Uncommon.
Range: Bermuda; North Carolina; Florida south to West Indies to Venezuela; Texas; Mexico; Surinam; southern Brazil.
Remarks: Shell said to be rare, but at times can be picked up by bushelfuls along Mexican coast just south of Rio Grande; syn. *C. poulsenii* Mörch, 1877.

Subgenus *Monoplex* Perry, 1811

Von Salis' Triton
Cymatium (Monoplex) parthenopeum
(Von Salis, 1793)

Size: Up to 90 mm.
Color: Usually light brownish yellow; may have spiral bands of slightly darker brown becoming darker on varices.
Shape: Conic with extended siphonal canal.
Ornament or sculpture: 7 to 8 postembryonic whorls; convex; shouldered; spire moderately extended; suture slightly indented; spiral sculpture

consists of 5 or 6 broad, low, often nodulose cords, with many finer threads in interspaces and on cords; transverse sculpture of fine growth lines with 2 low varices in adults.

Aperture: Subelliptical; outer lip bordered with paired teeth opposite grooves between external spiral cords; parietal wall dark reddish brown with numerous, irregular, white plications; anal canal bordered with ridge on parietal wall; short siphon, upturned, with columella extending into it at parietal margin

Habitat: Below low water to 63 meters (35 fathoms); epifaunal.

Localities: Entire.

Occurrence: Fairly common to uncommon.

Range: Bermuda; North Carolina; Florida; Texas; Mexico; West Indies; Surinam south to Brazil; Uruguay; Indo-Pacific; Japan.

Remarks: Syn. *C. costatum* Born, 1778; found on both sides of Panama.

Genus *Distorsio* Röding, 1798
Subgenus *Rhysema* Clench & Turner, 1957

Atlantic Distorsio
Distorsio (Rhysema) clathrata
  (Lamarck, 1816)

sculpture consists of numerous low cords interspaced with fine spiral threads; transverse sculpture of numerous cords that cross spiral cords, producing reticulated pattern with small knobs at point of crossing; 7 to 9 varices.

Aperture: Auriculate with thickened outer lip; outer lip has 10 denticles, third below anal canal largest and opposite deep parietal embayment; inner lip has numerous plicae; 2 large parietal plicae border posterior canal; spiral cords thickened in parietal embayment, continuing as plicae on columella, which is nearly straight and upturned; wide, thinly glazed parietal shield bordered by thin varix ridge.

Habitat: Just below low water to 54 meters (30 fathoms) in warm seas; epifaunal.

Localities: Entire.

Occurrence: Uncommon.

Range: Southeastern United States; Gulf states; Campeche Bank; Caribbean; Surinam; Brazil.

Remarks: Distorted aperture basis for name.

Size: 25–75 mm.
Color: Grayish white.
Shape: Conic with siphonal canal.
Ornament or sculpture: 10 irregular, convex whorls; spire extended; suture slightly impressed, irregular; spiral

Suborder SIPHONOSTOMATA Blainville,
1824 = [STENOGLOSSA Troschel, 1848,
and NEOGASTROPODA Thiele, 1925]
Superfamily CANCELLARIACEA Gray,
1853
Family CANCELLARIIDAE Forbes &
Hanley, 1853

Genus *Cancellaria* Lamarck, 1799

Common Nutmeg
Cancellaria reticulata (Linné, 1758)

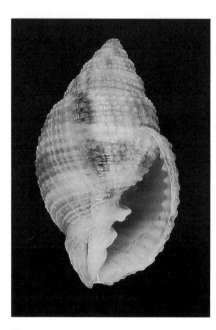

Remarks: Occasionally white specimens.

Superfamily CONACEA Rafinesque, 1815
Family TURRIDAE H. & A. Adams, 1853
Subfamily CRASSISPIRINAE

Genus *Crassispira* Swainson, 1840
Subgenus *Crassispirella* Bartsch &
Rehder, 1939

Oyster Turret
Crassispira (Crassispirella) tampaensis
Bartsch & Rehder, 1939 [See *SST*, p. 135]

Subfamily MANGELIINAE Fischer, 1883

Genus *Kurtziella* Dall, 1918
Subgenus *Kurtziella* s.s.

Brown-Tipped Mangelia
Kurtziella (Kurtziella) cf. *K. atrostyla*
(Tryon, 1884) [See *SST*, p. 136]

Waxen Mangelia
Kurtziella (Kurtziella) cf. *K. cerina* (Kurtz
& Stimpson, 1851)

Size: 2.54–3 cm.
Color: Cream background with mottlings
and irregular bands of reddish brown.
Shape: Conical with globose body whorl.
Ornament or sculpture: About 6 very
convex whorls. Sutures distinct. Body whorl
large; whorls of spire gradually decreasing
in size toward apex.
Aperture: Lunate, canal short, columella
with oblique folds. No operculum.
Habitat: Shallow sands and grass to several
fathoms.
Localities: Entire.
Occurrence: Locally common.
Range: North Carolina; Florida to Texas;
West Indies; Brazil.

Size: 9 mm.
Color: Waxen white to ash color on upper
whorls; no lines of color.
Shape: Turriculate.
Ornament or sculpture: Spire equal to last
whorl; 5 postnuclear whorls, flattish,
angulated on shoulder; small larval whorls,
smooth except for last, which has 4
nodulous spiral lines; granulous spiral

sculpture; 9 swollen transverse riblets; no varix; suture adpressed, undulated.

Aperture: Narrow, oblique, about one-half length of body whorl; notch well marked, away from suture; canal very short.

Habitat: Mud flats between tides; hypersaline lagoons and inlet areas; epifaunal [?].

Localities: Entire.

Occurrence: Fairly common in beach drift.

Range: Massachusetts; North Carolina; both sides of Florida; Texas.

Remarks: Specimens usually worn and difficult to identify; [*Mangelia cerina*].

Punctate Mangelia
Kurtziella (Kurtziella) cf. *K. limonitella* (Dall, 1884)

Size: 9 mm.

Color: Whitish, lineated spirally with yellow brown; some brown on outside of canal.

Shape: Turriculate.

Ornament or sculpture: Spire trifle shorter than last whorl; 5 postnuclear whorls, rounded angulated near periphery; spiral sculpture granulose; 12 narrow, transverse riblets; no varix; ribs obsolete on fasciole; suture hardly adpressed or undulated.

Aperture: Narrow, oblique; notch shallow, deepest at angulation; canal not distinct from aperture.

Habitat: Offshore banks and mud flats between tides; hypersaline lagoons and inlets; epifaunal [?].

Localities: Entire.

Occurrence: Fairly common.

Range: North Carolina to both sides of Florida; Texas.

Remarks: Does not have little beads on last nuclear whorl that *K. cerina* has; [*Drillia limonitella*], [*Mangelia limonitella*]. [Figured specimen in *SST*, p. 137, is *Cryoturris* cf. *C. Cerinella* (Dall, 1889)].

Subgenus *Rubellatoma* Bartsch & Rehder, 1939

Reddish Mangelia
Kurtziella (Rubellatoma) cf. *K. rubella* (Kurtz & Stimpson, 1851) [See *SST*, p. 138]

Genus *Cryoturris* Woodring, 1828

Wax-Colored Mangelia
Cryoturris cf. *C. cerinella* (Dall, 1889)

Size: 10.5 mm.

Color: Whitish toward apex, ashy on intermediate, orangish on body whorl; never striped or spotted.

Shape: Turriculate, drawn out, slender.

Ornament or sculpture: 7 postnuclear whorls, angulate at periphery and sloping either way from it; granulose spiral sculpture; 6 or 7 transverse ribs; suture less adpressed and undulated than *Kurtziella cerina*.

Aperture: Long, narrow, oblique; hardly any indentation for notch; no canal to speak of.
Habitat: Mud flats between tides; hypersaline lagoons and inlets; epifaunal [?].
Localities: Entire.
Occurrence: Common.
Range: North Carolina to both sides of Florida; Texas.
Remarks: Beach specimens very worn; [*Kurtziella cerinella*].

Genus *Nannodiella* Dall, 1919

Nannodiella cf. *N. vespuciana*
(Orbigny, 1842)

Size: 5 mm.
Color: Yellowish white, tinged with brown just below suture and on anterior part of body whorl.
Shape: Fusiform.
Ornament or sculpture: 8 postnuclear whorls strongly angulated just below middle, ornamented with about 9 rather prominent, straight transverse ribs, commencing at periphery and extending to suture; these, with their wide, concave interspaces, are crossed by 3 strong, rounded, equally distant threads, the third defining suture; where these cross ribs, nodules are formed; nucleus smooth, glassy; surface granulose.

Aperture: Narrow ovate, pinched up anteriorly into short, rather narrow, straight canal; outer lip thickened, with conspicuous varix and thick, smooth, rounded, irregularly curved, light brown edge; deep, narrow sinus considerably below suture, at angle of shoulder; columella slightly curved.
Habitat: Probably offshore; epifaunal [?].
Localities: Entire.
Occurrence: Uncommon in beach drift.
Range: North Carolina; Gulf states.
Remarks: Syn. *Mangelia oxytata* Bush, 1885

Genus *Pyrgocythara* Woodring, 1928

Plicate Mangelia
Pyrgocythara plicosa (C. B. Adams, 1850)

Size: 6–8 mm.
Color: Reddish brown; dead shells wax colored.
Shape: Turriculate; spire about one-half length.
Ornament or sculpture: 6 to 7 whorls; sutures distinct; only slightly shouldered; spiral sculpture of strong, regularly spaced cords; 11 to 12 transverse ribs made nodulose by spiral cords.
Aperture: Semilunar; outer lip thickened with very pronounced posterior notch below suture; interior dark; parietal lip narrow; siphonal canal short.
Habitat: Shallow, hypersaline lagoon on grass or mud bottom; epifaunal [?].

Localities: Entire.
Occurrence: Common.
Range: Cape Cod to western Florida; Texas.
Remarks: Posterior notch eases identification; [*Mangelia plicosa*].

Family TEREBRIDAE Mörch, 1852

Genus *Terebra* Bruguière, 1792
Common Atlantic Auger
Terebra dislocata (Say, 1822)

Size: 37–51 mm.
Color: Grayish white to orangish white.
Shape: Turriculate.
Ornament or sculpture: Numerous slightly convex whorls with about 15 axial ribs per whorl; sutures distinct with beaded spiral band just below and fine spiral striae between ribs.
Aperture: Small, subovate; outer lip thin with recurved siphonal notch at base; columella short; narrow parietal area polished.
Habitat: Inlet areas; infaunal.
Localities: Entire.
Occurrence: Common.
Range: Maryland to Florida; Texas; West Indies; Brazil.

Remarks: Can be found under bulges of sand at low tides.

Flame Auger
Terebra taurinus (Lightfoot, 1786)

Size: 100–150 mm.
Color: Background cream with axial reddish brown, flame-shaped marks in two spiral rows.
Shape: Turriculate, slender.
Ornament or sculpture: About 14 flattened whorls; sutures distinct; 2 spiral incised lines between sutures; numerous fine, wavy transverse striations.
Aperture: Semilunar, oblique, short; thin outer lip; columella convexly curved; anterior or siphonal canal short, recurved.
Habitat: Deeper water offshore; infaunal.
Localities: Southeast.
Occurrence: Uncommon.
Range: Southeastern Florida; Gulf of Mexico; West Indies; Surinam; Brazil.
Remarks: Syn. *T. flammea* Lamarck, 1822.

Subgenus *Strioterebrum* Sacco, 1891

Fine-Ribbed Auger
Terebra (Strioterebrum) protexta
(Conrad, 1846)

Genus Hastula H. & A. Adams, 1853

Sallé's Auger
Hastula salleana Deshayes, 1859

Size: 20–25 mm.
Color: Brownish when living.
Shape: Turriculate.
Ornament or sculpture: 13 to 15 slightly convex whorls; suture distinct; spiral sculpture of band below suture similar to but less pronounced than *T. dislocata;* convex, axial riblets crossed by fine spiral striations.
Aperture: Small, oblique, oval; outer lip thin; parietal area narrow, glossy; columella short with upturned siphonal notch at base.
Habitat: Offshore in 1.8–90 meters (1–50 fathoms); inlet areas; infaunal.
Localities: Entire.
Occurrence: Fairly common.
Range: North Carolina to Florida; Texas; Campeche Bank; Yucatán; Caribbean; Brazil.
Remarks: Terebra is Latin for a boring tool or auger.

Size: 25–51 mm.
Color: Dark bluish gray or brownish; polished.
Shape: Elongate conic.
Ornament or sculpture: Numerous flat-sided whorls; sutures distinct; apex very pointed; about 30 short, dark ribs below suture of each whorl; spiral sculpture of microscopic rows of punctuations, more widely spaced than in *H. cinera* Born, 1780.
Aperture: Small, pear-shaped, dark brown within; outer lip thin, with deep siphonal notch at base; sharp ridge runs from notch to mid-columella.
Habitat: Sandy surf zone; infaunal.
Localities: Northwest.
Occurrence: Common.
Range: Florida west to Veracruz, Mexico; Colombia; Brazil.
Remarks: During warm months in surf zone with *H. maryleeae* Burch and *Donax* clams; fed on by starfish, *Luida clathrata;* [*Terebra salleana*]; has been listed as *T. cinerea* Born, 1780.

Family BUCCINIDAE Rafinesque, 1815

Genus *Cantharus* Röding, 1789

Cancellate Cantharus
Cantharus cancellarius (Conrad, 1846)

Genus *Pisania* Bivona, 1832

Tinted Cantharus
Pisania tincta (Conrad, 1846)

Size: 18–28 mm.
Color: Yellowish brown.
Shape: Ovate conic.
Ornament or sculpture: 5 to 6 convex, heavy whorls; spire conical; spiral sculpture of sharp cords that form beads and cross narrow transverse ribs, making reticulate pattern.
Aperture: Long oval, glossy white; outer lip thin, crenulate with fine denticulations on inner edge; posterior canal weak or absent; siphonal canal straight, short, slightly upturned; one plica at base of columella.
Habitat: Shallow water in rocky places, inlet areas; epifaunal.
Localities: Entire.
Occurrence: Fairly common.
Range: Western coast of Florida to Texas; Yucatán.
Remarks: Lives on jetties and rocks.

Size: 18–28 mm.
Color: Variable: blue gray, yellow, chocolate, milk white; darkest at apex.
Shape: Ovate conic.
Ornament or sculpture: 5 to 6 convex, heavy whorls; spire conical; spiral sculpture of cords with finer threads in between, crossing over weak axial ribs; weak nodules on whorl shoulder.
Aperture: Oval; outer lip thickened, denticulate on inner edge; parietal lip glazed; plica on upper part borders small posterior or abaxial canal; siphonal canal almost straight, slightly upturned.
Habitat: Shallow water, rocks, seaweed close to shore; epifaunal.
Localities: Entire.
Occurrence: Fairly common.
Range: North Carolina to both sides of Florida; Texas; Campeche Bank; West Indies; eastern Brazil.
Remarks: Alive on jetties; dead in rolls of sea whip coral; [*Cantharus tinctus*].

Family NASSARIIDAE Iredale, 1916

Genus *Nassarius* Dumeril, 1806
Subgenus *Nassarius* S.S.

Sharp-Knobbed Nassa
Nassarius (Nassarius) acutus (Say, 1822)

Common Eastern Nassa
Nassarius (Nassarius) vibex (Say, 1822)

Size: 6–12 mm.
Color: Cream white to yellowish,
occasionally with brown spiral thread.
Shape: Ovate conic.
Ornament or sculpture: 7 convex whorls;
spire pointed and longer than body whorl;
spiral sculpture of spiral threads that cross
similar transverse ribs, giving beaded,
cancellate appearance to shell.
Aperture: Oval, slightly oblique; short
recurved siphonal canal.
Habitat: Open lagoon, inlet, along shore;
semi-infaunal.
Localities: West.
Occurrence: Common.
Range: Western coast of Florida to Texas.
Remarks: This scavenger attracted by smell
of decaying flesh and by light; feeds on
debris, other mollusks, and mollusk egg
capsules; lays eggs in gelatinous capsules
attached to bottom; young *Anadara
brasiliana* attach with byssus to shell of *N.
acutus* in symbiotic relationship.

Size: 12 mm.
Color: Gray brown to whitish with a few
splotches of darker brown.
Shape: Ovate conic.
Ornament or sculpture: 7 convex whorls;
body whorl dominates short, heavy shell;
spiral sculpture of fine threads that cross
about 12 transverse ribs; sutures shallow;
apex acute.
Aperture: Oval, small; outer lip with thick
varix, denticulate within; columella arched,
short; parietal area well developed, glazed
white; siphonal canal short, slightly
upturned.
Habitat: In bay and open-sound margins
and inlet areas; semi-infaunal.
Localities: Entire.
Occurrence: Common.
Range: Cape Cod to Florida; Gulf states;
Costa Rica; West Indies; Brazil.
Remarks: These scavenging "mud snails"
common on flats but most move to deeper
water in winter; eggs laid in gelatinous
capsules attached to bottom.

Family FASCIOLARIIDAE Gray, 1853
Subfamily FASCIOLARIINAE Gray, 1853

Genus *Fasciolaria* Lamarck, 1799
Subgenus *Fasciolaria* s.s.

Banded Tulip Shell
Fasciolaria (Fasciolaria) lilium
    Fischer von Waldheim, 1807

shaped capsules attached to shell, pilings, and other structures; referred to as *F. hunteria* Perry, 1811.

True Tulip Shell
Fasciolaria tulipa (Linné, 1758)

Size: 51–100 mm.
Color: Background cream with irregular purplish brown and orange brown mottlings; widely spaced, rarely broken, brown spiral bands.
Shape: Elongate fusiform.
Ornament or sculpture: 7 to 9 rounded whorls; smooth near well-defined sutures; spiral striations on base and fine transverse growth lines.
Aperture: Long oval, glazed white inside; outer lip thin, brownish with numerous raised white threads on inner surface; parietal area thinly glazed with white; moderately long siphonal canal open; incurved columella has strong plication toward end.
Habitat: Inlet areas and offshore; epifaunal.
Localities: Entire.
Occurrence: Common.
Range: North Carolina to western Gulf of Mexico.
Remarks: Uses its strong foot to jump out of unwary collector's pocket; eggs in vase-

Size: 7.5–12.5 cm.
Color: Cream background with brown blotches and numerous broken spiral bands. Some specimens reddish, orange, or mahogany brown.
Shape: Elongate, fusiform.
Ornament or sculpture: About 9 rounded whorls; suture distinct. Smooth appearing but has fine spiral striae just below suture and on base. Transverse sculpture consists of fine, irregular growth lines.
Aperture: Long oval, flushed with orangish color. Outer lip thin, denticulate on the inner edge. Parietal area thinly glazed. Columella fairly long, curved inward with 2 oblique plicae about midway. Operculum, corneous, unguiculate.
Habitat: Grass bottoms from littoral to 5 fathoms. Epifaunal.
Localities: Entire.

Occurrence: Common.
Range: Off Carolinas to the Gulf of Mexico; Caribbean; Brazil.
Remarks: The living animal is a bright flame color. More common in Keys.

Genus *Pleuroploca* P. Fischer, 1884

Florida Horse Conch
Pleuroploca gigantea (Kiener, 1840)

Size: Up to 150–225 mm.
Color: Dirty white to chalky salmon; juveniles bright orange.
Shape: Fusiform.
Ornament or sculpture: About 8 convex whorls; sutures distinct; spiral sculpture of strong, irregularly spaced cords, with finer threads between; transverse growth lines.
Aperture: Oval, polished, orange colored; outer lip thin, slightly crenulate; columella has 2 plicae near base; siphonal canal long, upturned.
Habitat: Offshore and in inlet areas; epifaunal.
Localities: Entire.
Occurrence: Fairly common.
Range: North Carolina to both sides of Florida; Texas; Campeche Bank.

Remarks: Old specimens usually covered with calcareous bryozoa; faded and worn even when living. This is the state shell of Florida.

Family MELONGENIDAE Gill, 1871 = [GALEODIDAE Thiele, 1925]

Genus *Melongena* Schumacher, 1817

Common Crown Conch
Melongena corona (Gmelin, 1791)

Size: 7 cm.
Color: Variable, cream with wide spiral bands of purplish brown.
Shape: Ovate with short spire; large inflated body whorl.
Ornament or sculpture: Variable, shoulder and base with 1 to 4 rows of semitubular spines that may point either horizontally or vertically.
Aperture: Wide, oval; deep recurved notch at base; outer lip simple. Operculum corneous, oval; dark brown.
Habitat: Mangroves and oysters in sheltered bays with muddy bottoms.
Localities: Entire.

Occurrence: Common.
Range: Florida; the Gulf States; Mexico.
Remarks: M. *melongena* (Linné, 1758) is a heavier species in the Greater Antilles.

Subfamily BUSYCONINAE Finlay & Marwick, 1937

Genus *Busycon* Röding, 1798
Subgenus *Busycoartum* Hollister, 1958
Turnip Whelk
Busycon coartatum (Sowerby, 1825)

Size: 12.5–15.24 cm.
Color: Cream background with purplish-brown vertical streaks.
Shape: Turnip-shaped.
Ornament or sculpture: Short spines may be present on shoulders.
Aperture: Wide, extending into a long, open siphonal canal. Operculum corneous, unguiculate.
Habitat: Moderately shallow water.
Localities: West.
Occurrence: Uncommon to rare.
Range: Southwest Gulf of Mexico, Gulf of Campeche.

Remarks: Once considered rare. Still highly sought-after. Usually dredged.

Subgenus *Fulguropsis* E. S. Marks, 1850
Pear Whelk
Busycon spiratum (Lamarck, 1822)

Size: 7.6–12.7 cm.
Color: Cream with longitudinal reddish-brown streaks.
Shape: Pyriform.
Ornament or sculpture: Strong spiral ridges; beaded shoulders on early whorls. Suture channeled with a deep v-shaped groove; inner face almost vertical.
Aperture: Wide; straight, open canal. Operculum corneous, oval; dark brown.
Habitat: Shallow areas from littoral to 4 fathoms.
Localities: Entire.
Occurrence: Common.
Range: North Carolina to both sides of Florida.
Remarks: Syn. *B. pyrum* (Dillwyn, 1817). Not as long and narrow as the thinner *B. s. plagosum* (Conrad, 1863).

Family COLUMBELLIDAE Swainson,
1840 = [PYRENIDAE Suter, 1913]

Genus *Anachis* H. & A. Adams, 1853
Subgenus *Costoanachis* Sacco, 1890

Semiplicate Dove Shell
Anachis (Costoanachis) semiplicata
Stearns, 1873

Subgenus *Parvanachis* Radwin, 1968

Fat Dove Shell
Anachis (Parvanachis) ostreiocola
Sowerby, 1882

Size: 8–15 mm.
Color: Yellow gray or whitish with reddish
brown, irregular markings.
Shape: Fusiform.
Ornament or sculpture: Spire slightly more
than one-half of shell length; whorls almost
flat-sided; sutures shallow; body whorl
narrow; sculpture of small number of
widely spaced, low axial ribs limited to
body whorl; spire smooth.
Aperture: Moderately wide; outer lip barely
thickened, distinctly denticulate interiorly;
columella straight with obsolete
denticulations.
Habitat: On broken shell and rocks in
sandy areas; epifaunal.
Localities: West; Keys.
Occurrence: Common.
Range: Southwestern Florida; Gulf of
Mexico to Progreso, Yucatán.
Remarks: Turn old shells and rocks to find
this tiny beauty.

Size: 4–5 mm.
Color: Variable: some whitish with dark
brown bands, others solid reddish brown.
Shape: Ovate conic; short fusiform.
Ornament or sculpture: 5 convex whorls,
stout, rotund; spiral sculpture of strong
spiral cords that do not cross transverse
ribs, giving reticulated pattern.
Aperture: Oval, oblique; outer lip
thickened in adults with denticulations on
inner edge; base of columella denticulate.
Habitat: Under shell on sandy bottoms and
oyster reefs; epifaunal.
Localities: Northwest.
Occurrence: Common.
Range: Bermuda; Virginia to Florida; Gulf
states; Costa Rica; West Indies; Surinam;
Brazil.
Remarks: *A. ostreicola* is probably a variety
of *A. obesa;* they differ in the proportion of
body whorl to spire. *A. ostreicola* has less
flaring apertural lip, greater overall
convexity of spire, uniform and distinct
overall color pattern, and stronger spiral
sculpture; lives on oyster reefs in shallow
mudbottom areas, whereas *A. obesa* prefers
deeper water on sand bottoms; *A.
ostreicola* ranges Gulf of Mexico for Key
West, Florida, to South Texas.

Genus *Mitrella* Risso, 1826
Subgenus *Astyris* H. & A. Adams, 1853

Lunar Dove Shell
Mitrella *(Astyris) lunata* (Say, 1826)

Size: 5 mm.
Color: Glossy white to cream with numerous fine, zigzag brown markings; occasional specimens have brown markings in definite spiral bands.
Shape: Ovate conic.
Ornament or sculpture: Smooth with about 5 flat-sided, tapering whorls; spiral striations on base of shell.
Aperture: Long oval; outer lip thin on edge, denticulated on interior; columella short; edge of siphonal canal dark brown.
Habitat: High-salinity shell reef just below low-tide mark, grass flats, inlets; epifaunal.
Localities: Entire.
Occurrence: Common.
Range: Bermuda; Massachusetts to Florida; Texas; Carmen, Campeche, Mexico; Gulf of Campeche; Yucatán; West Indies; Surinam; northern and northeastern Brazil.
Remarks: Some marked below sutures in spiral bands of white followed by brown dots and oblique lines; may belong in genus *Anachis,* subgenus *Alia.*

Family MURICIDAE Rafinesque, 1815
Subfamily MURICINAE da Costa, 1776

Genus Murex Linné, 1758

Cabrit's Murex
Murex cabritii Bernardi, 1859

Size: 5–5.5 cm.
Color: Unicolor, yellow, white, or rose pink.
Shape: Conic with inflated body whorl, spire short. Long, slim, straight siphonal canal.
Ornament or sculpture: 3 rows of 3 to 7 long slender spines; 3 rounded, spinose varices per whorl.
Aperture: Small, oval; outer lip crenulate. Operculum brown, corneous.
Habitat: 18 to 70 fathoms.
Localities: South.
Occurrence: Uncommon.
Range: Southeastern United States to the West Indies; Gulf of Mexico.
Remarks: Syn. *M. maculatus* Verill, 1950. Spines are usually broken on beach specimens.

Rose Murex
Murex rubidus F. C. Baker, 1897

Size: 4 cm.
Color: Variable; cream, pink; brownish pink to salmon and red; often with brown bands.
Shape: Conic with inflated body whorl, spire acute. Extended, straight siphonal canal.
Ornament or sculpture: Spines short or absent, often recurved; 3 spines on columellar side of canal.
Aperture: Obliquely ovate. Operculum corneous, oval; dark brown.
Habitat: On coral rubble bottom from 2 to 39 fathoms.
Localities: Southeast, southwest; Keys.
Occurrence: Uncommon.
Range: Southeastern United States and the Bahamas.
Remarks: Similar to *M. cabritii* Bernardi with fewer spines and shorter canal.

Subgenus *Hexaplex* Perry, 1810

Giant Eastern Murex
Murex (Hexaplex) fulvescens G.B. Sowerby I, 1834

Size: 125–150 mm.
Color: Milky white to dirty gray with reddish brown blotches with spiral threads.
Shape: Conic; extended siphonal canal.
Ornament or sculpture: 6 to 7 convex, heavy whorls; suture distinct, irregular; spire short; spiral sculpture of strong, brown cords that connect corresponding spines to each varix, numerous raised threads between them; transverse sculpture of 6 to 10 highly spinous varices.
Aperture: Oval to subcircular; outer lip crenulated, thickened into very spinose varix; parietal lip glazed with low ridge at upper part; siphonal canal fairly short, broad; previous canals form series of flutings terminating in false umbilicus; interior porcelaneous white.
Habitat: On jetties and just offshore or in inlet areas; semi-infaunal.
Localities: East, southeast.
Occurrence: Common.
Range: North Carolina; Florida to Texas; northern Mexico.
Remarks: Deposits eggs in rubbery capsules attached to some substratum; larvae have nonpelagic development.

Subgenus *Phyllonotus* Swainson, 1833

Apple Murex
Murex (Phyllonotus) pomum
(Gmelin, 1791)

Range: North Carolina to Florida; Texas; Campeche Bank; Yucatán; West Indies; Surinam; Brazil.
Remarks: This carnivore bores into shell of prey; eggs deposited in yellowish, leathery, tongue-shaped, massed capsules; old shells occupied by hermit crabs occasionally found in inlet areas.

Subgenus *Chicoreus* Momfort, 1810

Lace Murex
Chicoreus dilectus A. Adams, 1855

Size: 51–112 mm.
Color: Dark brown to yellowish tan with irregular dark brown spiral bands, which are often reduced to spots.
Shape: Conic with slightly extended siphonal canal.
Ornament or sculpture: 7 to 9 solid, convex whorls; suture not always distinct; spire extended; spiral sculpture of series of strong cords; scaly cords form nodules on ridges, several finer scaly threads between them; transverse sculpture of 3 prominent, equidistant varices on each whorl; each varix has row of low, open spines and fluted edge on forward margin; several ridges between varices.
Aperture: Oval to subcircular, large; interior polished, colored pink or ivory, yellow, orange; outer lip thin, crenulate with varix bordering outer edge; spotted brown to correspond with spiral bands; parietal area glazed, adheres to body whorls, except for erect edge; siphon short, slightly recurved; dark brown spot on upper end of parietal wall.
Habitat: Gravelly bottom, 5.4 to 12.6 meters (3 to 7 fathoms); semi-infaunal.
Localities: Entire.
Occurrence: Common.

Size: 5 cm.
Color: Light brown or whitish.
Shape: Conic with inflated body whorl, extended spire. Extended, straight siphonal canal.
Ornament or sculpture: 8–10 scaly, frondlike spines closely set along outer lip and siphonal canal.
Aperture: Small, nearly round. Operculum, round brown, corneous.
Habitat: Varied; shallow mangrove, muddy areas, and clear sandy areas.
Localities: Southeast.
Occurrence: Common.

Range: Southeastern United States to Florida.

Remarks: Syn. *M. arenarius* Clench & Farfante, 1945

Subfamily PURPURINAE Menke, 1828

Genus *Urosalpinx* Stimpson, 1865

Gulf Oyster Drill
Urosalpinx perrugata (Conrad, 1846)

Size: 2.5 cm.
Color: Grayish or yellow-white with irregular brown bands.
Shape: Somewhat fusiform, sturdy.
Ornament or sculpture: 6–9 axial ribs which are quite large at periphery. Strong spiral cords.
Aperture: Ovate, rosy-brown; outer lip thickened on the inside with 6 small, white teeth. Operculum corneous, ovate.
Habitat: Intertidal on mud flats.
Localities: Entire.
Occurrence: Common.
Range: Florida.
Remarks: Lays its purse-shaped eggs on *Busycon* or *Fasciolaria* egg cases.

Genus *Purpura* Bruguière, 1798

Wide-Mouthed Purpura
Purpura patula (Linné, 1758)

Size: 5 cm.
Color: Dull rusty gray. Columella salmon-pink.
Shape: Ovate.
Ornament or sculpture: Low pointed nodules arranged spirally on body whorl.
Aperture: Large, smooth, narrow columella; outer lip with brownish-black stain. Operculum corneous.
Habitat: Intertidal rocks.
Localities: Southeast.
Occurrence: Common to uncommon.
Range: Southeast Florida; West Indies; Bermuda.
Remarks: The animal produces a harmless purple dye.

Subfamily THAIDINAE Suter, 1913

Genus *Thais* Röding, 1798
Subgenus *Stramonita* Schumaker, 1817

Hays' Rock Shell
*Thais (Stramonita) haemastoma
canaliculata* (Gray, 1839)

floridana; in other areas this mollusk
serious oyster pest.

Florida Rock Shell
Thais (Stramonita) haemastoma floridana
(Conrad, 1837)

Size: Up to 112 mm.
Color: Grayish with irregular mottling of
darker color in either axial or spiral pattern.
Shape: Conic.
Ornament or sculpture: 7 to 8 convex,
solid whorls; sutures usually indented; body
whorl has angled shoulder; spiral sculpture
of numerous coarse, incised lines with 2
rows of large nodules on whorl shoulder;
transverse sculpture of fine growth lines.
Aperture: Subovate; outer lip thickened
with crenulations that run into aperture;
interior light brownish to pinkish orange;
parietal lip glazed, thickened by inductura;
ridge at upper edge runs into aperture; may
be weak plicae on base of straight
columella; siphonal canal short, oblique;
umbilicus closed.
Habitat: Shallow water on rocks or oyster
reefs; epifaunal.
Localities: Entire.
Occurrence: Fairly common.
Range: Bermuda; Gulf of Mexico from
Florida west to Texas.
Remarks: *T. h. canaliculata* and *T. h.
haysae* may only be variations of *T. h.*

Size: 51–75 mm.
Color: Light gray to yellowish, mottled
with darker color in axial pattern.
Shape: Conic.
Ornament or sculpture: 6 to 7 convex
whorls. Sutures in rather heavy shell fine,
occasionally indented; sculpture quite
variable; spiral sculpture may consist of
incised lines and 2 rows of small nodules;
transverse sculpture of fine growth lines;
shoulders may be angled or not.
Aperture: Subovate; interior salmon pink;
outer lip dark brown between
denticulations that run into interior of
aperture; parietal lip glazed, smooth,
thickened by inductura; columella straight,
may have faint plicae near base; anal canal
short with ridge along parietal wall;
siphonal canal short, oblique; umbilicus
closed.
Habitat: Intertidal on rocks; epifaunal.
Localities: Entire.
Occurrence: Common.

Range: North Carolina to Florida; Texas; Yucatán; Central America; West Indies; northern and northeastern Brazil.
Remarks: Carnivorous on bivalves; lays eggs in purplish capsules clustered together on rocks, cans, bottles, etc.

Subfamily ASPELLINAE Keen, 1971

Genus *Favarita* Jousseaume, 1880
Pitted Murex
Favarita cellulosa (Conrad, 1846)

Genus *Thais* Röding, 1798
Rustic Rock Shell
Thais rustica (Lamarck, 1822)

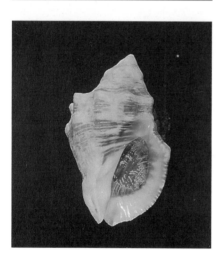

Size: 2.5 cm.
Color: Dull grayish white.
Shape: Conical, solid.
Ornament or sculpture: Rough; 5 to 7 poorly developed fluted varices. Short, upturned siphonal canal.
Aperture: Small, almost round. Operculum corneous, brown, unquiculate.
Habitat: Subtidal rocks near oyster beds.
Localities: Southeast.
Occurrence: Common.
Range: Carolinas to East Brazil; Bermuda.
Remarks: Syn. *Murex jamaicensis* Sowerby, 1879

Size: 2.5 cm.
Color: Dull rusty gray, spirally banded with brown.
Shape: Conical, solid.
Ornament or sculpture: 1 or more rows of nodules on shoulder and mid-area of whorl.
Aperture: Parietal wall glossy white with brown spots on crenulated outer lip. Operculum corneous.
Habitat: Intertidal rocks and coral.
Localities: Southeast.
Occurrence: Common.
Range: Southeast Florida; West Indies and Bermuda; Brazil.
Remarks: Look for the white columella and purple stain at lower, inner corner.

Superfamily VOLUTACEA
Rafinesque, 1815
Family OLIVIDAE Latreille, 1825
Subfamily OLIVINAE Swainson, 1840

Genus *Oliva* Bruguière, 1789
Subgenus *Ispidula* Gray, 1847

Lettered Olive
Oliva (Ispidula) sayana Ravenel, 1834

Netted Olive
Oliva reticularis Lamarck, 1810

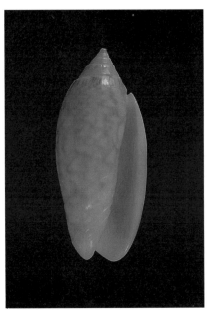

Size: 51–62 mm.
Color: Polished cream-colored background with numerous brownish zigzag markings.
Shape: Elongate oval.
Ornament or sculpture: 5 to 6 whorls; body whorl dominates shell; spire short, acute; sutures deep.
Aperture: Long, narrow, purplish within; outer lip thin; siphonal canal oblique notch at base; white columella plicated.
Habitat: Inlets and offshore; infaunal.
Localities: Entire.
Occurrence: Common.
Range: North Carolina to Florida; Gulf states; West Indies; Brazil.
Remarks: Skin divers find this nocturnal predator plowing along just under sand; shell covered with propodium and lateral folds of foot; in warm months feeds on *Donax,* occasionally on *Polinices duplicatus,* in winter reduces feeding and depends on scavenging.

Size: 5 cm.
Color: Variable; ground color whitish with yellowish to dark brown reticulations.
Shape: Cylindrical.
Ornament or sculpture: Smooth, glossy; columella with weak spiral lines.
Aperture: White, long narrow. No operculum.
Habitat: Off coral sand beaches on sandy bottom.
Localities: Southeast; Keys.
Occurrence: Common.
Range: Southeast Florida to East Brazil; Bermuda.
Remarks: Because color is so variable a number of color forms have been described.

Genus *Olivella* Swainson, 1831
Whitened Dwarf Olive
Olivella dealbata (Reeve, 1850)

Family TURBINELLIDAE Swainson, 1840
Subfamily VASINAE H. & A. Adams, 1854

Genus *Vasum* Röding, 1798
Caribbean Vase
Vasum muricatum (Born, 1778)

Size: 6–9 mm.
Color: Glossy white or cream; body whorl faintly marked with brownish zigzag streaks; color variable.
Shape: Elongate oval.
Ornament or sculpture: Smooth; sutures distinct, slightly canaliculated; fasciole at base of shell white, bounded with fine raised thread.
Aperture: Long, narrow, about three-fourths length of body whorl; outer lip thin; parietal inductura well developed; columella slightly concave with 7 to 9 weak oblique plications; siphonal notch not as pronounced as in *O. minuta.*
Habitat: Inlet areas in sand; infaunal.
Localities: West.
Occurrence: Common.
Range: North Carolina to both sides of Florida; Texas; Yucatán; West Indies.
Remarks: At times in winter months can be found by thousands in drift on outer beaches; closely related to *O. floralia* Duclos, 1835, and may be only a form of it.

Size: 8 cm.
Color: Dull-white, covered with heavy brown periostracum.
Shape: Ovate-conic, heavy.
Ornament or sculpture: Spiral cords and axial nodes or blunt spines at shoulder.
Aperture: Large, elongate, shiny-white, usually tinged with purple. Heavy corneous operculum.
Habitat: Near reefs and rocky bottom, shallow water.
Localities: Southeast.
Occurrence: Common.
Range: Southeast Florida to West Indies.
Remarks: Often found in pairs.

Family VOLUTIDAE Rafinesque, 1815
Subfamily SCAPHELLINAE H. & A.
Adams, 1858

Genus *Scaphella* Swainson, 1832

Junonia
Scaphella junonia (Lamarck, 1804)

Family MARGINELLIDAE Fleming, 1828

Genus *Prunum* Herrmannsen, 1852
Subgenus *Leptegouana* Woodring, 1928

Common Atlantic Marginella
Prunum (Leptegouana) apicina Menke,
1828

Size: 5–9 cm.
Color: Pinkish ivory with spiral rows of
mahogany-red squarish dots.
Shape: Elongate-ovate, 5 whorls; apex
rounded.
Ornament or sculpture: Smooth.
Aperture: Elongate, notched at base,
outerlip simple, sharp; columella involute,
with 4 oblique folds. No operculum.
Habitat: Offshore on rocky reefs.
Localities: Entire.
Occurrence: Uncommon on beach.
Range: North Carolina to both sides of
Florida; Mexico.
Remarks: A very sought-after shell that is
commonly caught by scallop trawlers.
Animal is spotted.

Size: 12 mm.
Color: Polished cream, yellowish, or
grayish tan with several reddish brown
spots on outer lip.
Shape: Conic, broad anteriorly.
Ornament or sculpture: Smooth; spire
short; convex body whorl large.
Aperture: Long, narrow, length of body
whorl; outer lip thickened, notched at base;
columella with 4 strong plicae below.
Habitat: Shallow, grassy, inlet-influenced
areas; epifaunal.
Localities: Entire.
Occurrence: Common.
Range: North Carolina to Florida; Gulf
states; Yucátan; West Indies.
Remarks: [*Marginella apicina*].

Family CONIDAE Rafinesque, 1815

Genus *Conus* Linné, 1758

Sozon's Cone
Conus delessertii Récluz, 1843

Alphabet Cone
Conus spurius atlanticus Gmelin, 1791

Size: 6.38–10.46 cm.
Color: Variable; orange with conspicuous white bands with spiral rows of brownish dots.
Shape: Conical with slightly concave elevated spire; apex sharp.
Ornament or sculpture: 10–12 spiral ridges at lower end of shell.
Aperture: Long, narrow; outer lip sharp. Operculum not observed.
Habitat: Deeper water.
Localities: Entire.
Occurrence: Uncommon.
Range: Off Carolinas to the Gulf of Mexico; Bermuda.
Remarks: Commonly taken by scallop trawlers; beach specimens rare. Syn. *C. sozoni* Bartsch, 1939.

Size: 5.08–7.62 cm.
Color: Creamy white with spiral rows of squarish brown and orange spots.
Shape: Conical.
Ornament or sculpture: Spiral bands are less distinct than *C. spurius* of the West Indies.
Aperture: Long, narrow; inner lip with slight spiral ridges on lower margin. Operculum chitinous, narrow, one-half length of aperture.
Habitat: Subtidal in sand.
Localities: Southeast, south; Keys.
Occurrence: Fairly common.
Range: Florida and Gulf of Mexico.
Remarks: Similar to *C. proteus* Hwass of the Indian Ocean. Orange-banded form is rare.

Mesh-Pitted Chiton

Keyhole Limpet

Sculptured Top-Shell

Checkered Pheasant

Antillean Nerite

Olive Nerite

Virgin Nerite

Emerald Nerite

Angulate Periwinkle

Marsh Periwinkle

Zebra Periwinkle

Cloudy Periwinkle

Common Sundial

Atlantic Modulus

Plicate Horn Shell

Florida Cerith

Muddy Cerith

Mitchell's Wentletrap

White Wentletrap

Angulate Wentletrap

Humphrey's Wentletrap

Brown-Banded Wentletrap

Dwarf Purple Sea Snail

Common Purple Sea Snail

Globe Purple Sea Snail

Fighting Conch

Common Atlantic Slipper Shell

Eastern White Slipper Shell

Atlantic Deer Cowrie

Sea Whip Simnia

Shark's Eye

Brown Moon Shell

Colorful Atlantic Natica

Maculated Baby's Ear

Common Baby's Ear

Scotch Bonnet

Giant Tun Shell

Knobbed Triton

Gold-Mouthed Triton

Atlantic Hairy Triton

Poulsen's Triton

Von Salis' Triton

Atlantic Distorsio

Common Nutmeg

Common Atlantic Auger

Flame Auger

Fine-Ribbed Auger

Marylee's Terebra

Sallé's Auger

Cancellate Cantharus

Tinted Cantharus

Common Eastern Nassa

Banded Tulip Shell

True Tulip Shell

Florida Horse Conch

Semiplicate Dove Shell

Lunar Dove Shell

Giant Eastern Murex

Apple Murex

Florida Rock Shell

Lettered Olive

Whitened Dwarf Olive

Minute Dwarf Olive

Common Atlantic Marginella

Striate Bubble

Coffee Melampus

Striped False Limpet

Mossy Ark

Turkey Wing

White Miniature Ark

Doc Bales' Ark

Incongruous Ark

Cut-Ribbed Ark

Blood Ark

Ponderous Ark

Hooked Mussel

Tulip Mussel

Paper Mussel

Ribbed Mussel

Half-Naked Pen Shell

Saw-Tooth Pen Shell

Atlantic Pearl Oyster

Atlantic Wing Oyster

Rough Scallop

Calico Scallop

Lion's Paw

Atlantic Thorny Oyster

Atlantic Thorny Oyster
(beach specimen)

Common Jingle Shell

Spiny Lima

Thick Lucina

Eastern Oyster

Tiger Lucina

Buttercup Lucina

Florida Lucina

True Spiny Jewel Box

Broad-Ribbed Cardita

Prickly Cockle

Yellow Cockle

Common Egg Cockle

Morton's Egg Cockle

Giant Atlantic Cockle

Fragile Atlantic Mactra

Common Rangia

Atlantic Surf Clam

Smooth Duck Clam

Channeled Duck Clam

Jackknife Clam

DeKay's Dwarf Tellin

Alternate Tellin

White Crested Tellin

Constricted Macoma

Atlantic Sanguin

Purplish Semele

Purplish Tagelus

Carolina Marsh Clam

Calico Clam

Sunray Venus

Disk Dosinia

Elegant Dosinia

Cross-Barred Venus

Lady-in-Waiting Venus

Southern Quahog

Campeche Angel Wing

Angel Wing

Common Spirula

Florida Cone
Conus floridanus Gabb, 1868

Stearn's Cone
Conus jaspideus stearnsi Conrad, 1869

Size: 4–4.6 cm.
Color: Variable; usually white or buff with long, rather wide blotches of yellow to light yellow orange.
Shape: Conical, spire elevated and slightly concave; apex sharp.
Ornament or sculpture: Spiral bands of yellowish brown and white.
Aperture: Long, narrow; inner lip with slight spiral ridges on lower margin. Operculum not observed.
Habitat: Intertidal to 7 fathoms.
Localities: Entire.
Occurrence: Common.
Range: North Carolina to Florida.
Remarks: *C. f. floridensis* Sowerby, 1870 is a much darker color form with dotted reddish-brown spiral bands.

Size: 1.3–3 cm.
Color: Grayish to purple brown with spiral bands of tiny white and brown dots and darker yellowish brown streaks or blotches.
Shape: Conical, sturdy; spire high, slender.
Ornament or sculpture: Smooth; 8 stepped whorls.
Aperture: Long, narrow with deep, wide posterior notch. Operculum narrow, small, chitinous.
Habitat: Shallow water to 30 feet in sand or grass.
Localities: Entire.
Occurrence: Moderately common.
Range: North Carolina; Florida to Yucatán.
Remarks: Intergrades with *C. jaspideus.*

Jasper Cone
Conus jaspideus Gmelin, 1791

Size: 1.3–3 cm.
Color: Variable; white with irregular patches of reddish brown.
Shape: Conical, sturdy; spire almost half of length; keeled shoulder.
Ornament or sculpture: 10 stepped whorls, prominent spire, apex sharp; regularly spaced spiral lines.
Aperture: Long, narrow. Operculum narrow, small, chitinous.
Habitat: Shallow water in sand.
Localities: South.
Occurrence: Common.
Range: North Carolina, Florida to Texas; West Indies; Brazil.
Remarks: Formerly listed as *C. peali* Green. It has many synonyms. The black speckled yellow animal lays its eggs inside dead ark shells.

Subclass EUTHYNEURA Spengel, 1881 = [OPISTHOBRANCHIA Milne Edwards, 1848, and PULMONATA Cuvier, 1817]
Order SACOGLOSSA Von Ihering, 1876 = [ASCOGLOSSA Bergh, 1877]

Order DORIDOIDEA Odhner, 1934 = [HOLOHEPATICA Bergh, 1881]
Suborder CRYPTOBRANCHIA Fischer, 1883 = [EUDORIDOIDEA Odhner, 1934]
Superfamily DORIDACEA Rafinesque, 1815
Family DORIDIDAE Rafinesque, 1815
Subfamily DISCODORIDINAE Bergh, 1891

Genus *Discodoris* Bergh, 1877
Discodoris hedgpethi Marcus & Marcus, 1959 [See *SST*, p. 156]

Suborder PHANEROBRANCHIA Von Ihering, 1876
Superfamily ONCHIDORIDACEA Alder & Hancock, 1845 = [SUCTORIA Bergh, 1892]
Family CORAMBIDAE Bergh, 1869

Genus *Doridella* Verrill, 1870
Doridella obscura Verrill, 1870 [See *SST*, p. 157]

Order DENDRONOTOIDEA
Odhner, 1936
Family SCYLLAEIDAE Rafinesque, 1815

Genus *Scyllaea* Linné, 1758
Sargassum Nudibranch
Scyllaea pelagica Linné, 1758

Order EOLIDOIDEA Odhner, 1937
Suborder EOLIDOIDEA Odhner, 1968
Infraorder ACLEIOPROCTA
Odhner, 1939
Family FIONIDAE Gray, 1837

Genus *Fiona* Forbes & Hanley, 1851
Atlantic Blue Fiona
Fiona pinnata (Eschscholtz, 1831)

Size: 25–51 mm.
Color: Yellowish brown to orange brown, *Sargassum* colored.
Shape: Sluglike.
Ornament or sculpture: No oral tentacles; 2 slender, long rhinophores; 2 series of large foliaceous gill plumes, or cerata, on each side of body.
Aperture: None.
Habitat: Pelagic in *Sargassum;* epifaunal.
Localities: Entire.
Occurrence: Common with *Sargassum.*
Range: Southeastern United States; other warm seas.
Remarks: Found clinging to *Sargassum,* along with at least 4 other unidentified nudibranchs; will live in aquarium for days, a delight to watch; eggs laid in zigzag, yellow gelatinous strings.

Size: 39 mm.
Color: Variable: reddish, bluish, yellowish.
Shape: Sluglike.
Ornament or sculpture: Margins of foot broad, extending beyond body sides; cerata densely situated along margins of notum, leaving large part of back clear; each of larger cerata has conspicuous longitudinal membrane along posterolateral axis, containing undulating blood vessel.
Aperture: None.
Habitat: Pelagic on floating seaweed.
Localities: Entire.
Occurrence: Seasonally common.
Range: Gulf Stream; Alaska to Peru.
Remarks: Brought in by spring winds; feeds on *Velella* coelenterates and *Lepas* barnacles; syn. *F. nobilis* (Alder & Hancock, 1848).

Infraorder CLEIOPROCTA Odhner, 1939
Family FAVORINIDAE Bergh, 1889
Subfamily FAVORININAE Bergh, 1889

Genus *Cratena* Bergh, 1864
Cratena pilata Gould, 1870 [See *SST*, p. 158]

Family EOLIDIIDAE Orbigny, 1834

Genus *Spurilla* Bergh, 1864
Spurilla neapolitana (Delle Chiaje, 1823)

Range: Florida to Texas; Caribbean to Brazil; eastern Atlantic; Mediterranean.
Remarks: First collected in Texas by Joel W. Hedgpeth at Port Aransas on June 25, 1948; feeds on sea anemones.

Genus *Berghia* Trinchese, 1877
Berghia coerulescens (Laurillard, 1831) [See *SST*, p. 159]

Genus *Cerberilla* Bergh, 1873
Cerberilla tanna Marcus & Marcus, 1959 [See *SST*, p. 160]

Family GLAUCIDAE Menke, 1828

Genus *Glaucus* Forster, 1777
Blue Glaucus
Glaucus atlanticus Forster, 1777

(after E. du B.-R. Marcus and E. Marcus, *Pub. Inst. Marine Sci.* 6:251–254 [1959])

Size: 20–40 mm.
Color: Colorful, varying from ivory, yellowish rose, or pinkish with reddish brown to olive green diverticula within cerata, which are tipped with white and keeled on side facing midline; opaque white dots on cerata, head, back.
Shape: Elongate, tapered posteriorly; sluglike.
Ornament or sculpture: Rows of arched cerata on dorsal surface.
Aperture: None.
Habitat: On weeds attached to floating logs; pelagic.
Localities: Probably entire.
Occurrence: Occasionally common.

Size: 51 mm.
Color: Shades of blue.
Shape: Sluglike body.
Ornament or sculpture: Tentacles and rhinophores small; 4 clumps of bright blue frilled cerata on each side of body.
Aperture: None.
Habitat: Pelagic in warm seas.
Localities: Entire.
Occurrence: Occasionally common.
Range: Worldwide.

Remarks: This brightly colored slug washed ashore by strong southeast winds in spring when *Janthina* coming in; feeds on siphonophores.

Suborder BULLOIDEA Lamarck, 1801
Superfamily BULLACEA Lamarck, 1801
Family BULLIDAE Lamarck, 1801

Genus *Bulla* Linné, 1758
Striate Bubble
Bulla striata Bruguière, 1792

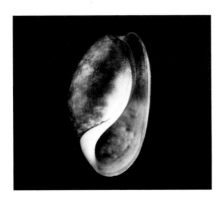

Size: 18–25 mm.
Color: Whitish with small irregular mottlings of chocolate brown.
Shape: Oval with sunken spire.
Ornament or sculpture: Delicate shell smooth except for microscopic growth lines; spiral sculpture of fine grooves toward base and within sunken apical end.
Aperture: Longer than body whorl, wider near base; interior whitish; outer lip thin; parietal area covered with glazed white inductura.
Habitat: Inlet areas on grass in shallow water; epifaunal.
Localities: Entire.
Occurrence: Common.
Range: Bermuda; western coast of Florida to Texas; Yucatán; Costa Rica; West Indies to Brazil.
Remarks: Mantle of this carnivore completely envelops shell; photosensitive;

burrows in grass roots; eggs in gelatinuous ribbons.

Family ACTEOCINIDAE Pilsbry, 1921

Genus *Aceteocina* Gray, 1847
Channeled Barrel-Bubble
Acteocina candei (d'Orbigny, 1841)

Size: 3.6 mm.
Color: Glossy white.
Shape: Cylindrical with moderately elevated spire.
Ornament or sculpture: Smooth except for axial ribbing on sub-sutural band.
Aperture: Long, narrow, wider at base; outer lip thin; columella single, raised fold below parietal inductura.
Habitat: Near-shore oceanic conditions.
Localities: Entire.
Occurrence: Common in beach drift.
Range: Cape Hatteras to Florida; Texas; Campeche Bank; West Indies; Surinam.
Remarks: Gelatinous egg masses attached to marine grasses; nonpelagic veligers; [*Retusa canaliculata*].
More cylindrical and much smaller than the common *A. canaliculata* Say, 1826, an extremely similar and often confused estuarine species.

Orbigny's Baby-Bubble
Acteocina bidentata (Orbigny, 1841)

Family ATYIDAE Thiele, 1926

Genus *Haminoea* Turton & Kingston, 1830
Conrad's Paper-Bubble
Haminoea succinea (Conrad, 1846)

Size: 2.5–4 mm.
Color: White, fragile.
Shape: Cylindrical.
Ornament or sculpture: Smooth; spire depressed; body whorl narrowed above and below.
Aperture: Long, narrow; outer lip thin, slightly flared below; columella short with 2 plicae at base.
Habitat: Inlet areas near low-water mark; infaunal.
Localities: Entire.
Occurrence: Fairly common.
Range: North Carolina; Florida; Gulf states; Yucatán; West Indies; Brazil.
Remarks: Maculated mantle of this minute carnivore envelops shell; crawls just under sand leaving a raised trail. Syn. *Cylinchnella bidentata.*

Size: 10 mm.
Color: White to pale amber.
Shape: Cylindrical, thin; spire insunk.
Ornament or sculpture: Surface covered with minute, wavy, spiral lines.
Aperture: Longer than body whorl, wider near base; outer lip thin, sharp; columella concave with one weak fold above center.
Habitat: Inlet influence in shallow water; epifaunal.
Localities: West.
Occurrence: Uncommon.
Range: Bermuda; Florida to Texas; Campeche Bank.
Remarks: Animal brown.

Genus *Volvulella* Newton, 1891

Volvulella persimilis (Mörch, 1875) [See *SST*, p. 164]

Suborder APLYSIOIDEA Lamarck, 1809
Infraorder LONGICOMMISSURATA
    Pruvot-Fol, 1954
Superfamily ALPLYSIACEA Lamarck, 1809
Family APLYSIIDAE Rafinesque, 1815
Subfamily APLYSIINAE Rafinesque, 1815

Genus *Aplysia* Linné, 1767
Subgenus *Varria* Eales, 1960

Mottled Sea Hare
Aplysia (Varria) brasiliana Rang, 1828

(swimming)

Size: 100–225 mm.
Exudate: Reddish purple.
Shell: Narrow to broad, concave, dark yellow, with apex hard and hooked but without spire; internal.
Body: Very variable; large, bulky, self-colored or spotted; tough skin; simple cephalic tentacles; slender rhinophores set close together; long neck; narrow foot; long tapering verge; very large parapodia joined low down posteriorly; mantle aperture tubular; opaline gland compound, uniporous; simple radula.
Habitat: Bays and offshore reefs where algae grows; epifaunal.
Localities: Entire.
Occurrence: Common.
Range: New Jersey to Brazil; St. Helena; Ghana.
Remarks: Syn. *A. floridensis* (Pilsbry, 1895) and *A. willcoxi* Helprin, 1886; more abundant in warm months; does well in aquariums; eggs deposited in tangled mass of gelatinous ribbons on grass flats, usually dark green to light brown; currently subject of expanded field and laboratory culture studies because of importance in neurophysiological and behavioral studies.

(G. W. Tryon, Jr., *Manual of Conchology* [Philadelphia: Acad. Natur. Sci., 1895] 16:pl. 35)

(inner shell)

Spotted Sea Hare
Aplysia (Varria) dactylomela Rang, 1828

Sooty Sea Hare
Aplysia (Varria) morio Verrill, 1901

(after P. C. S. A. L. Rang, "Histoire naturelle des Aplysiens . . . ," in *Histoire naturelle gen. et partic. des mollusques-pteropodes*, ed. Ferussac [1828], pl.9)

Size: 100–125 mm.
Exudate: Deep purple.
Shell: Large, broad, rounded, with oblique apex; strongly calcified, with hardly any trace of spire; internal.
Body: Bulky; basic yellowish green color, with numerous large black rings of irregular sizes on sides; thick rhinophores with short notched apices; broad foot with blunt tail; frilled swimming lobes joined low down posteriorly; broad spatulate spirally grooved verge; compound uniporous opaline gland; lateral teeth of radula with long straight smooth cusps.
Habitat: Where algae grow abundantly; epifaunal.
Localities: South.
Occurrence: Common.
Range: Circumtropical.
Remarks: Syn. *A. protea* Rang, 1828; lifespan 1 year.

Size: 212–318 mm.
Exudate: Purple.
Shell: Long and narrow without spire, strongly ridged, hardly any anal sinus; internal.
Body: Bulky; dark purple to black; wide hemispherical tentacles; narrow foot with short tail; very large, free, thin, swimming parapodia, arising close behind rhinophores, becoming wide, rounded and fluted on edges, uniting low down on tail; mantle and visceral regions small; no shell foramen in adult; large leaflike siphon, large cteniduium, simple multiporous opaline gland; radula with numerous rows and more than 50 teeth on each side; elaborate denticulation; verge sheath anchored by numerous muscle strands, plain internally; verge short, stout, unpigmented.
Habitat: Where algae grow abundantly; epifaunal.
Localities: Entire.
Occurrence: Common sporadically during summer.
Range: Rhode Island to Texas; Bermuda and the West Indies.
Remarks: Excellent swimmer.

Infraorder BREVICOMMISSURATA
Pruvot-Fol, 1954
Subfamily DOLABRIFERINAE Pilsbry,
1895

Genus *Bursatella* Blainville, 1817

Ragged Sea Hare
Bursatella leachii pleii (Rang, 1828)

(Tryon 1895, 16:pl. 43)

Size: 100 mm.
Exudate: Not defined.
Body: Olive green to gray, usually with
white specks; covered with numerous
ragged appendages.
Shell: None in adult.
Habitat: Where algae grow abundantly.
Localities: Entire.
Occurrence: Fairly common.
Range: Worldwide circumtropical.
Remarks: First reported in Texas by Breuer
(1962); form common to Gulf of Mexico;
just one of a number of subspecies.

Order ENTOMOTAENIATA
Cossmann, 1896
Superfamily PYRAMIDELLACEA
Gray, 1840
Family PYRAMIDELLIDAE Gray, 1840

Genus *Pyramidella* Lamarck, 1799
Subgenus *Longchaeus* Mörch, 1875

Notched Pyram
Pyramidella (Longchaeus) crenulata
(Holmes, 1859)

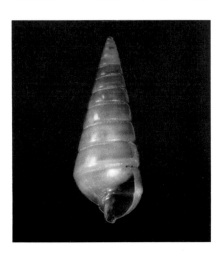

Size: 10–12 mm.
Color: Pale brown; cream to white when
dead; polished.
Shape: Elongate conic.
Ornament or sculpture: Numerous flat-
sided whorls; sutures distinct, V-shaped
channels; spire acute; body whorl rounded
at base; posterior margin of each whorl
delicately crenulated; weak basal line meets
outer lip at suture; phaneromphalous.
Aperture: Small, rather auriform, entire;
outer lip thin; columella sinuous, 2 oblique
folds.
Habitat: Ectoparasitic in inlets and
hypersaline lagoons; epifaunal.
Localities: Entire.
Occurrence: Common.
Range: South Carolina to Florida; Texas;
West Indies.
Remarks: One of the largest pyrams.

Genus *Boonea* Robertson, 1978

Impressed Odostome
Boonea impressa (Say, 1822)

Half-Smooth Odostome
Boonea seminuda (C. B. Adams, 1839)

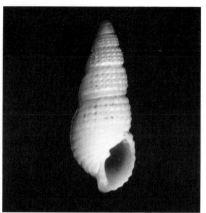

Size: 4–6 mm.
Color: Whitish.
Shape: Elongate conic.
Ornament or sculpture: 8 flattened whorls, shouldered above; sutures channeled; nuclear whorls small, partly imbedded in first succeeding turn; spiral sculpture of 3 strong deeply cut grooves; grooves cut by spiral threads; base rounded, spirally grooved.
Aperture: Ovate; outer lip thin, slightly sinuous at edge, showing external sculpture within; columella stout with strong oblique plica at insertion.
Habitat: Ectoparasitic on oyster reefs; epifaunal.
Localities: Entire.
Occurrence: Common.
Range: New Jersey to Quintana Roo.
Remarks: Most common *Boonea* on Texas coast; because it feeds on *Crassostrea virginica*, this ectoparasite has been studied considerably; also feeds on *Diastoma*, *Crepidula*, and oyster drills; according to Robert Robertson, the Texas species may be different from the one in North Carolina, although they seem to have identical shells; a North Carolina population has pelagic larvae, while a Texas population has nonpelagic larvae; probably syn. *Odostomia trifida* Totten, 1834; [*Odostomia impressa*].

Size: 4 mm.
Color: Whitish.
Shape: Elongate conic.
Ornament or sculpture: 6 to 7 slightly convex whorls; whorls shouldered; sutures distinct; whorls sculptured between sutures by axial ribs cancellated into beads or nodules by 4 low, broad, equidistant ridges; base of body whorl spirally grooved.
Aperture: Auriform; outer lip thick inside but edge thin, entire; columella strong, twisted, reflexed with oblique plica.
Habitat: Ectoparasitic in bays and on shallow shelf; epifaunal.
Localities: Entire.
Occurrence: Fairly common.
Range: Prince Edward Island, Canada, to Texas.
Remarks: Nonspecific ectoparasite known to feed on *Crepidula* and *Pecten;* can stand less saline waters than some of the other *Boonea;* holes in dead specimens indicate that gastropods feed on it in turn.

Genus *Fargoa* Bartsch, 1955
Fargoa cf. *F. bushiana* (Bartsch, 1909)

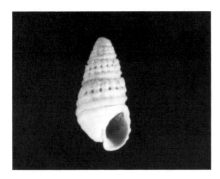

Size: 1.8–3 mm.
Color: White.
Shape: Elongate conic.
Ornament or sculpture: 4 postnuclear whorls; each whorl bears 3 rows of tubercles and smooth spiral keel just above suture.
Aperture: Obliquely oval or pear-shaped; 1 plica on columella.
Habitat: Ectoparasitic in bays; epifaunal.
Localities: Entire.
Occurrence: Rare.
Range: Massachusetts to São Paulo, Brazil.
Remarks: Called *Odostomia dux* in *SST*, p. 171, but *O. dux* is not a synonym; it is a name that has been misapplied to the species.

Fat Odostome
Fargoa gibbosa (Bush, 1909)

Size: 3 mm.
Color: Whitish, polished.
Shape: Globose conic.
Ornament or sculpture: About 5 very convex whorls; shell rather fragile; sutures distinct; smooth except for microscopic growth striations.
Aperture: Pear-shaped, fairly large; outer lip thin; columella marked with single prominent tooth near insertion.
Habitat: Ectoparasitic in inlet areas; epifaunal.
Localities: Undetermined.
Occurrence: Undetermined.
Range: Connecticut; North Carolina; Louisiana; Texas.
Remarks: Rounded shape of shell distinguishes it from other *Fargoa*. Reported ranges indicate it has to be in Florida. Search!

Genus *Odostomia* Fleming, 1817
Subgenus *Evalea* A. Adams, 1860
? *Odostomia (Evalea)* cf. *O. emeryi* (Bartsch, 1955)

Size: 2.9 mm.
Color: Cream yellow.
Shape: Elongate conic.
Ornament or sculpture: Thin; nuclear whorls small, obliquely immersed in first postnuclear turn; postnuclear whorls well rounded and crossed by numerous microscopic spiral lines; suture deeply impressed; base inflated, rounded, strongly umbilicated.

Aperture: Large, oval; columella slender, curved with internal spiral cord near insertion; parietal wall covered with thin inductura; outer lip thin, strongly curved; rounded body whorl distinctive.
Habitat: Uncertain.
Localities: Northwest.
Occurrence: Fossil.
Range: Undetermined; known from Pliocene of North St. Petersburg, Florida.
Remarks: Fold on columella places species among *Pyramidellas*, but has not been definitely identified.

Genus *Sayella* Dall, 1885

? Sayella cf. *S. livida* Rehder, 1935

Size: 3.5–4 mm.
Color: Straw yellow with wide subsutural white band.
Shape: Elongate conic.
Ornament or sculpture: About 6 ½ moderately convex whorls; smooth except for microscopic growth lines and spiral sculpture; whorls closely adpressed at suture; body whorl half of shell length, suture considerably below periphery of preceding whorl.
Aperture: Small, obliquely ovate; lip thin, thickened anteriorly, proceeding into base of columella, which bears a strong fold; area surrounding base of columella reddish brown.
Habitat: Ectoparasitic in bays and inlet areas; epifaunal.
Localities: Not determined.
Occurrence: Not determined.

Range: Florida; Texas.
Remarks: Identification only a guess if correct, holotype collected by J. A. Singley in Corpus Christi Bay, Texas, in 1893.

Sayella sp.

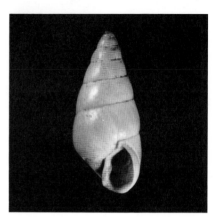

Size: 3–5 mm.
Color: Translucent grayish white alive; opaque white to brownish dead.
Shape: Ovate conic.
Ornament or sculpture: 4 to 6 convex whorls; suture fairly impressed; spiral sculpture absent or microscopic; nuclear whorls impressed in apex; may have chinklike umbilicus; quite variable.
Aperture: Ovate; columellar tooth weak.
Habitat: Ectoparasitic in inlet-influenced areas, shallow water; epifaunal.
Localities: Not determined.
Occurrence: Not determined.
Range: Massachusetts to Texas.
Remarks: Species resembles *Odostomia laevigata* (Orbigny, 1842), which is primarily a West Indian species and does not range north to Massachusetts.

Genus *Peristichia* Dall, 1889
Peristichia toreta Dall, 1889

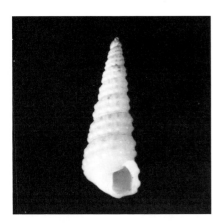

Size: 11 mm.
Color: White.
Shape: Elongate conic.
Ornament or sculpture: Spiral sculpture of 3 raised, rounded cords on upper whorls, 2 uppermost being nodulated, lower smooth; only 1 basal cord; columella without folds.
Aperture: Rounded.
Habitat: Shallow water.
Localities: Entire.
Occurrence: Uncommon.
Range: North Carolina to western Florida; Texas.
Remarks: Usually placed with *Turbonillas* but now considered separate.

Genus *Eulimastoma* Bartsch, 1916
Eulimastoma cf. *E. harbisonae* Bartsch, 1955 [See *SST*, p. 174]

Eulimastoma cf. *E. teres* (Bush, 1885)

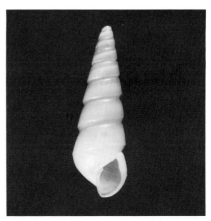

Size: 4.5 mm.
Color: White, lustrous.
Shape: Turreted.
Ornament or sculpture: About 7½ flattened whorls, sutures canaliculate; whorls have distinct, impressed, spiral line just below angle; body whorl distinctly angulated at periphery where there is a prominent, rounded thread, with somewhat elongated, rounded base; nucleus large, very oblique.
Aperture: Not so much produced anteriorly; in juveniles plica very conspicuous; umbilicus small, deep, nearly concealed by reflected inner lip.
Habitat: Ectoparasitic in low-salinity bays; epifaunal.
Localities: Not determined.
Occurrence: Not determined.
Range: Cape Hatteras; Texas.
Remarks: Suture variable; [*Odostomia teres*].

Genus *Turbonilla* Risso, 1826

According to Helmer Odé, author of a monograph in the *Texas Conchologist*, the genus *Turbonilla* may be restricted to the Atlantic Coast along New England. The shells depicted here were collected in Texas. They look similar to *Turbonilla* and *Chemitzia*. Use these IDs only as guides to locate these tiny shells.

Genus *Pyrgiscus* Philippi, 1841
Interrupted Turbonilla
Pyrgiscus cf. *interrupta* Totten, 1835

Occurrence: Undetermined.
Range: Main to West Indies; Texas; Carmen, Campeche, Mexico; Gulf of Campeche; Yucatán; Brazil.
Remarks: Disappearance of original shell described by Totten has contributed to misinterpretation of this species.

Genus *Strioturbonilla* Sacco, 1892
Hemphill's Turbonilla
Strioturbonilla cf. *hemphilli* Bush, 1899

Size: 6 mm.
Color: Brownish.
Shape: Elongate conic, slender.
Ornament or sculpture: About 10 almost flat whorls sculptured with about 22 smooth, axial ribs separated by grooves of a little wider width, and with about 14 subequal, impressed, revolving lines arranged in pairs and entirely interrupted by ribs; spiral line above periphery heavier than others, forming line of deep pits; ribs obsolete below middle of body whorl; base short, rounded with spiral lines.
Aperture: Ovate, angular above, regularly rounded below, about one-fifth length of shell; outer lip sharp, slightly sinuous; columella slightly curved, weakly reflexed.
Habitat: Ectoparasitic in inlets and along shore; epifaunal.
Localities: Probably entire.

Size: 10–12 mm.
Color: White.
Shape: Elongate conic, slender.
Ornament or sculpture: 12 postnuclear whorls slightly convex, sculptured with about 20 almost perpendicular transverse ribs; rounded ribs separated by about equally wide, deep, concave spaces ending at periphery of body whorl in clean-cut ends; base rounded, smooth; entire surface covered with microscopic striations.
Aperture: Squarish, somewhat expanded below; inner lip thickened, reflected.
Habitat: Ectoparasitic in inlet-influenced areas; epifaunal.
Localities: West.
Occurrence: Fairly common.
Range: Western coast of Florida; Texas.

Subfamily CYCLOSTREMELLINAE
D. Moore, 1966

Genus *Cyclostremella* Bush, 1897

Cyclostremella humilis (Bush, 1897) [See
SST, p. 180]

Order ACTOPHILA Thiele, 1931
Superfamily ELLOBIACEA Adams, 1855
Family ELLOBIIDAE Adams, 1855
Subfamily MELAMPINAE Stimpson, 1851

Genus *Melampus* Montfort, 1810

Coffee Melampus
Melampus bidentatus Say, 1822

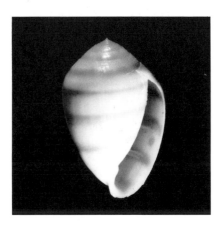

Size: 18 mm.
Color: Brown with cream-colored bands.
Shape: Ovate.
Ornament or sculpture: Rather thin shell smooth; about 5 whorls; spire low; body whorl predominates; omphalous.
Aperture: Nearly length of body whorl, expanded below; outer lip thin, curved into columella; columella short with 2 white plicae; internal lamellae inside body whorl.
Habitat: Under vegetation on bay and lagoon shores; epifaunal.
Localities: Southeast?
Occurrence: Common.
Range: Florida to West Indies; Texas.

Remarks: Examination of stomachs of wild ducks shows this snail to be a favorite food; only breeds in water.

Subfamily PEDIPEDINAE Thiele, 1931

Genus *Pedipes* Bruguière, 1792

Stepping Shell
Pedipes mirabilis (Mühlfeld, 1818)

Size: 3–5 mm.
Color: Light to dark reddish brown.
Shape: Globose turbinate.
Ornament or sculpture: 4 to 5 strongly convex whorls; sculpture of numerous incised, spiral lines; transverse sculpture of irregular growth lines; spire slightly elevated; anomphalous.
Aperture: Oval with outer edge thin but thickened on inside; parietal area has 3 well-developed denticulations, top one being largest; outer lip has one tooth directly opposite central plica.
Habitat: Jetties and rocks above tide line; epifaunal.
Localities: Southeast.
Occurrence: Common.

Range: Bermuda; Florida to West Indies; Texas; Costa Rica; northeastern Brazil.
Remarks: This air breather can withstand environmental changes, but entire colony disappears under extreme conditions; prefers hard substratum.

Order HYGROPHILA Férussac, 1821
Superfamily SIPHONARIACEA Gray, 1840
Family SIPHONARIIDAE Gray, 1840

Genus *Siphonaria* Sowerby, 1824

Striped False Limpet
Siphonaria pectinata (Linné, 1758)

Size: 25.6 mm.
Color: Whitish with numerous brown bifurcating lines.
Shape: Conic, limpet-shaped.
Ornament or sculpture: Sculpture of numerous fine radial threads.

Aperture: Large, circular; interior glossy.
Habitat: Rocks and jetties; epifaunal.
Localities: Southeast.
Occurrence: Common.
Range: Georgia; eastern Florida; Texas; Mexico; West Indies.
Remarks: Common on jetties of Texas coast; resembles true limpet, but animal air breather.

Order THECOSOMATA Blainville, 1824
Suborder EUTHECOSOMATA
  Meisenheimer, 1905
Superfamily SPIRATELLACEA
  Thiele, 1926
Family CUVIERIDAE Gray, 1840

Genus *Creseis* Rang, 1828

Straight-Needle Pteropod
Creseis acicula (Rang, 1828)

Size: 20–30 mm.
Color: White, translucent.
Shape: Elongated, straight cone.
Ornament or sculpture: Smooth, not coiled.
Aperture: Small, round.
Habitat: Pelagic, temperate and tropic seas.
Localities: Entire.

Occurrence: Common, seasonally, in beach drift.
Range: Worldwide.
Remarks: Looks like very fine tusk shell and easily overlooked; at times may come to shore by thousands.

Subfamily CAVOLINIINAE
H. & A. Adams, 1854

Genus *Diacria* Gray, 1850

Four-Toothed Cavoline
Diacria quadridentata (Blainville, 1821)
[See *SST*, p. 183]

Three-Spined Cavoline
Diacria trispinosa Blainville, 1821

behind that may or may not be broken off; longitudinally ribbed on ventral side.
Aperture: Compressed, thickened; under lip curved outward.
Habitat: Pelagic, temperate and tropical seas.
Localities: Entire.
Occurrence: Uncommon in beach drift.
Range: Atlantic; Gulf of Mexico.
Remarks: Tends to rid itself of long hind stalk that would hamper swimming; descends during day, rises at night to feed; both sides of Panama.

Genus *Cavolina* Abildgaard, 1791

Long-Snout Cavoline
Cavolina longirostris (Blainville, 1821)

Size: 10 mm.
Color: Whitish with chestnut-colored lips.
Shape: Lozenge-shaped with extended hind part.
Ornament or sculpture: Shell somewhat compressed with 3 straight spines, one on either side of aperture and longer one

Size: 4–9 mm.
Color: Translucent white.
Shape: Triangular when viewed from top.
Ornament or sculpture: Ventral face of shell nearly round, sculptured with faint concentric ridges; dorsal face longitudinally ribbed, extended in front into long, slightly

folded, depressed bead; lateral spines compressed; central spine short, truncated.
Aperture: Compressed, continued as fissure around side of shell.
Habitat: Pelagic, warm and tropical seas.
Localities: Entire.
Occurrence: Common in beach drift.
Range: Worldwide.
Remarks: Easily overlooked in beach drift because it does not resemble usual concept of sea shell.

Aperture: Compressed, continued as fissure around each side of shell.
Habitat: Pelagic, warm and tropical seas.
Localities: Entire.
Occurrence: Fairly common in beach drift.
Range: Worldwide.
Remarks: When living, butterfly-like wings entend from either side of the rostrum.

Uncinate Cavoline
Cavolina uncinata (Rang, 1829)

Size: 6–11 mm.
Color: Pale amber, translucent.
Shape: Shield-shaped when viewed from top.
Ornament or sculpture: Shell very inflated ventrally, surface delicately and regularly reticulated with fine, concentric ridges in front; dorsal face with 3 low, radiating ribs, turned downward and nearly evenly rounded at aperture; lateral spines compressed and curved backward; central spine short, stout, upcurved.

Class BIVALVIA Linné, 1758 = [PELECYPODA Goldfuss, 1820]

Subclass PALAEOTAXODONTA
  Korobkov, 1954
Order NUCULOIDEA Dall, 1889
Superfamily NUCULACEA Gray, 1824
Family NUCULIDAE Gray, 1824

Genus *Nucula* Lamarck, 1799
Atlantic Nut Clam
Nucula cf. *N. proxima* Say, 1822

Remarks: Look for this little clam near river mouths.

Superfamily NUCULANACEA
  H. & A. Adams, 1858
Family NUCULANIDAE
  H. & A. Adams, 1858

Genus *Nuculana* Link, 1807
Pointed Nut Clam
Nuculana acuta (Conrad, 1831)

Size: 6.5 mm.
Color: Whitish.
Shape: Obliquely trigonal; equivalve; inequilateral.
Ornament or sculpture: Sculpture of faint growth lines and light radiating striae; margins rounded; ventral margin crenate.
Hinge area: Angular with 12 comblike teeth anterior to umbones and 18 posterior.
Pallial line & interior: Inner surface pearly; adductor muscle scars but no pallial sinus.
Habitat: Sandy mud bottom; infaunal.
Localities: Entire.
Occurrence: Fairly common in beach drift.
Range: Bermuda; Nova Scotia to Florida; Texas.

Size: 10 mm.
Color: White.
Shape: Elongate with pointed posterior rostrum; equivalve; inequilateral.
Ornament or sculpture: Sculpture of well-defined concentric grooves that do not extend over ridge on rostrum.
Hinge area: Small triangular chondrophore and numerous chevron-shaped teeth on either side of umbo.
Pallial line & interior: Interior polished; palial sinus small, rounded.
Habitat: Sandy mud beyond low tide; infaunal.
Localities: Entire.
Occurrence: Fairly common in beach drift.

Range: Cape Cod to West Indies; Texas; Carmen, Campeche, Mexico; Gulf of Campeche; Campeche Bank.

Remarks: Less obese than *N. concentrica*; very variable; some may lack concentric sculpture.

Concentric Nut Clam
Nuculana concentrica Say, 1824

Size: 12–18 mm.

Color: Yellow white, semiglossy.

Shape: Rather obese and moderately rostrate; equivalve; inequilateral.

Ornament or sculpture: Adult shells appear smooth; have very fine, concentric growth lines on ventral half of valves; beaks and area just below smooth; radial ridge on rostrum smooth, not crossed by strong threads.

Hinge area: Numerous chevron-shaped teeth on either side of umbo.

Pallial line & interior: Pallial sinus small, rounded; polished.

Habitat: Sandy bottoms beyond low tide; infaunal.

Localities: Northwest.

Occurrence: Fairly common in beach drift.

Range: Northwestern Florida to Texas; Surinam.

Remarks: Syn. *N. eborea* Conrad, 1848.

Subclass PTERIOMORPHIA Beurlen, 1944
Order ARCOIDEA Stoliczka, 1871
Superfamily ARCACEA Lamarck, 1809
Family ARCIDAE Lamarck, 1809
Subfamily ARCINAE Lamarck, 1809

Genus *Arca* Linné, 1758
Subgenus *Arca* s.s.

Mossy Ark
Arca (Arca) imbricata Bruguière, 1789

Size: 25–38 mm.

Color: Whitish, concentrically marked with chestnut bown.

Shape: Rectangular; hinge long, straight; equivalve; inequilateral.

Ornament or sculpture: Numerous fine, irregular ribs crossed with growth lines giving a beaded appearance; posteriorly carinate; large ventral byssal gape.

Hinge area: Wide, flat; pear-shaped ligamental area between umbones; hinge margin straight with many small transverse teeth.

Pallial line & interior: Interior smooth, dull purplish; muscle scars connected by simple pallial line.

Habitat: On rocks or firm substratum; byssate epifaunal nestler.

Localities: Entire.

Occurrence: Common.

Range: North Carolina; Florida to West Indies; Texas; Campeche Bank; Costa Rica; Surinam; Brazil.

Remarks: Attaches with byssal threads; barely discernible unless movement of valves closing is seen; syn. *A. umbonata* Lamarck, 1819.

Subgenus *Arca* s.s. Linné, 1758

Turkey Wing
Arca (Arca) zebra (Swainson, 1833)

Size: 5 cm.
Color: Creamy white, streaked with chestnut brown zebra pattern.
Shape: Rectangular; hinge long, straight; equivalve; inequilateral.
Ornament or sculpture: Ventral margin with wide byssal notch opposite umbones; posterior margin sinuate. About 26 narrow, rounded ribs with finely ribbed, flat interspaces. Fine lamellar ridges across both ribs and interspaces.
Hinge area: Wide, flat ligamental area between umbones. Numerous small, transverse teeth.
Pallial line & interior: Interior smooth, white to purplish; strong muscle and simple pallial impressions.
Habitat: On rocks, shell, roots. Byssate epifaunal nestler.
Localities: Southeast, south; Keys.
Occurrence: Common.
Range: North Carolina, southeastern Florida, West Indies; Texas; Campeche Bank; Yucatán; northern Brazil.
Remarks: Panamic vicariant is *A. pacifica* (Sowerby, 1833).

Genus *Barbatia* Gray, 1847
Subgenus *Barbatia* s.s.

Red Brown Ark
Barbatia (Barbatia) cancellaria (Lamarck, 1819) [See *SST*, p. 188]

White Bearded Ark
Barbatia (Barbatia) candida
(Helbling, 1779)

Size: 25.4–50.8 mm.
Color: White.
Shape: Obliquely rectangular; hinge straight; equivalve; inequilateral.
Ornament or sculpture: Margins irregular; slight byssal gape on ventral edge; relatively thin for ark; numerous weak, slightly beaded ribs, those on posterior dorsal area being very strongly beaded; surface irregular.
Hinge area: Straight with narrow, lanceolate ligamental area between umbones, narrower than *Arca*; teeth not parallel, obliquely inclined to center.
Pallial line & interior: Interior white, smooth; pallial line simple with 2 muscle scars.
Habitat: On rocks beyond low tide; byssate epifaunal nestler.
Localities: Entire.
Occurrence: Fairly common.
Range: North Carolina to West Indies; Texas; Brazil.
Remarks: Very few hinge teeth for arks.

Subgenus *Acar* Gray, 1857

White Miniature Ark
Barbatia (Acar) domingensis (Lamarck, 1819)

Subgenus *Fugleria* Reinhart, 1937

Doc Bales' Ark
Barbatia (Fugleria) tenera (C. B. Adams, 1845)

Size: 12–18 m.
Color: White to cream.
Shape: Rectangular; surface irregular; equivalve; inequilateral.
Ornament or sculpture: Very distinctive, coarsely reticulated surface; shinglelike growth ridges.
Hinge area: Ligament long, narrow, posterior to beaks; chevron-shaped teeth; umbo curled to edge of hinge.
Pallial line & interior: Pallial line simple with 2 muscle scars.
Habitat: On rocks below low tide; semi-epifaunal.
Localities: Entire.
Occurrence: Common.
Range: North Carolina to Florida; Texas; Gulf of Mexico to Quintana Roo; Costa Rica; Lesser Antilles; Surinam; Brazil; Brazilian oceanic islands.
Remarks: Look in holes and crevices of rocks on jetties.

Size: 25–38 m.
Color: White.
Shape: Trapezoidal, rather fat; equivalve; nearly equilateral.
Ornament or sculpture: Thin shelled; numerous rather evenly, finely beaded, codlike ribs, stronger posteriorly; small byssal gape.
Hinge area: Ligamental area fairly wide at umbo, narrowing anteriorly; typical chevron teeth.
Pallial line & interior: Interior polished, white; pallial line simple with 2 muscle scars.
Habitat: Offshore; byssate epifaunal nestler.
Localities: Entire.
Occurrence: Fairly common.
Range: Lake Worth, Florida, to Texas; Caribbean; northern coast of South America.
Remarks: Specimen figured in *SST*, p. 189, may be *B. candida*; immature forms easily confused.

Subfamily ANADARINAE Reinhart, 1935

Genus *Anadara* Gray, 1847
Subgenus *Cunearca* Dall, 1898

Incongruous Ark
Anadara (Cunearca) brasiliana
(Lamarck, 1819)

Chemnitz's Ark
Anadara (Cunearca) chemnitzi
(Philippi, 1851)

Size: 25–38 mm.
Color: White.
Shape: Trigonal; left valve overlaps right; inequivalve; inequilateral.
Ornament or sculpture: 26 to 28 radial ribs visible, stronger at margins.
Hinge area: Umbones well separated; ligament area wide, excavated; oblique, comblike teeth smaller toward center.
Pallial line & interior: Interior white, polished; ribs visible and stronger at margins; pallial line simple with 2 muscle scars.
Habitat: Offshore in shallow water; infaunal.
Localities: West.
Occurrence: Common.
Range: Southeastern United States; Texas; West Indies; Surinam; Brazil.
Remarks: Attaches by byssus to *Nassarius acutus* in symbiotic relationship; syn. *A. incongrua* Say, 1822.

Size: 25.6 mm.
Color: White.
Shape: Trigonal; inequivalve; inequilateral.
Ornament or sculpture: 26 to 28 broad ribs, strongly recurved posteriorly, bearing barlike beads.
Hinge area: Umbones well separated, forward of center of ligamental area; comblike teeth smaller toward center.
Pallial line & interior: Interior white, polished; ribs visible; pallial line simple with 2 muscle scars.
Habitat: Offshore in shallow water; epifaunal.
Localities: South and West.
Occurrence: Uncommon in beach drift.
Range: Texas; Mexico; Greater Antilles to Brazil; Surinam.
Remarks: Adult similar to *A. brasiliana* but heavier and smaller; juveniles very different.

Subgenus *Setiarca* Olsson, 1961

Cut-Ribbed Ark
Anadara (Setiarca) floridana
   (Conrad, 1869)

Subgenus *Larkiania* Reinhart, 1935

Transverse Ark
Anadara (Larkiania) transversa (Say, 1822)

Size: 63.5–127 mm.
Color: White.
Shape: Obliquely rectangular; equivalve; inequilateral.
Ornament or sculpture: Very heavy shell; 35 square ribs, each marked with deep central groove that does not extend over umbones and is not present on more rounded posterior ribs.
Hinge area: Umbones incurved, flattened; hinge margin straight; numerous comblike teeth.
Pallial line & interior: Interior marked with delicate lines; margins crenulate; pallial line simple and 2 muscle scars well defined.
Habitat: Deeper water offshore; infaunal.
Localities: West.
Occurrence: Uncommon.
Range: Southeastern United States; Texas; Greater Antilles.
Remarks: Line down center of rib makes this large ark distinctive and separates it (somewhat doubtfully) from *A. baughmani* Hertlein, 1951, a species from farther offshore; formerly referred to as *A. secticostata* Reeve, 1844, which has a brown stain; *A. lienosa* Say, 1822, a similar fossil form.

Size: 12–36 mm.
Color: White.
Shape: Transversely oblong; left valve overlaps right; equivalve; inequilateral.
Ornament or sculpture: 30 to 35 rounded ribs per valve; ribs on left valve usually beaded, seldom so on right valve.
Hinge area: Long, narrow ligamental space separates umbones; numerous teeth perpendicular to hinge line.
Pallial line & interior: Interior polished; pallial line simple with 2 muscle scars.
Habitat: Littoral to 10.8 meters (6 fathoms); inlet-influenced areas and offshore; infaunal.
Localities: Entire.
Occurrence: Fairly common.
Range: South of Cape Cod to Florida; Texas to Carmen, Campeche, Mexico; Gulf of Campeche.
Remarks: Highly variable.

Subgenus *Lunarca* Reinhart, 1943

Blood Ark
Anadara (Lunarca) ovalis
(Bruguière, 1789)

Family NOETIIDAE Stewart, 1930
Subfamily NOETIINAE Stewart, 1930

Genus *Noetia* Gray, 1840
Subgenus *Eontia* MacNeil, 1938

Ponderous Ark
Noetia (Eontia) ponderosa (Say, 1822)

Size: 38–59 mm.
Color: White.
Shape: Roundish to ovate; equivalve; inequilateral.
Ornament or sculpture: Ribs have weak groove in center; strong intercostal ribs; left valve more heavily sculptured than right; no byssal gape.
Hinge area: Ligament very narrow; umbones close together; comblike teeth.
Pallial line & interior: Pallial line simple with 2 muscle scars; ribs visible on polished white interior.
Habitat: Just offshore; infaunal.
Localities: Entire.
Occurrence: Common.
Range: Cape Cod to West Indies; Gulf states; Costa Rica; Brazilian coast to Rocha, Uruguay.
Remarks: Animal bright red; syn. *A. campechiensis* Gmelin, 1791.

Size: 50.8–63.5 mm.
Color: White.
Shape: Trigonal; equivalve; inequilateral.
Ornament or sculpture: Heavy, thick shell; 32 flattened square ribs with fine line down center; posterior margin nearly straight, keeled; fine concentric intercostal sculpture absent from umbones.
Hinge area: Umbones well separated; sides of hinge area slope obliquely downward to straight margin; teeth comblike.
Pallial line & interior: Pallial line simple with 2 strong, raised muscle scars; no byssal threads in adults.
Habitat: Inlet areas and offshore on sandy botom; infaunal.
Localities: Entire.
Occurrence: Common.
Range: Virginia to Key West; Gulf of Mexico.
Remarks: Heavy, brown periostracum is worn off at the beaks.

Order MYTILOIDEA Férussac, 1822
Superfamily MYTILACEA
  Rafinesque, 1815
Family MYTILIDAE Rafinesque, 1815
Subfamily MYTILINAE Rafinesque, 1815

Genus *Brachidontes* Swainson, 1840
Subgenus *Brachidontes* s.s.

Scorched Mussel
Brachidontes (Brachidontes) exustus
  (Linné, 1758)

Size: 18–38 mm.
Color: Yellowish brown to dark brown;
interior metallic purple and white.
Shape: Moderately fan-shaped.
Ornament or sculpture: Numerous
rounded, radial ribs dividing near ventral
margin and eroded near umbones; slight
byssal gape in ventral margin.
Hinge area: 2 small teeth at anterior end; 5
to 6 tiny teeth on edge of shell at posterior
end, beyond ligament.
Pallial line & interior: Pallial line weak,
simple; posterior muscle scar larger than
anterior.
Habitat: On rocks or oyster reefs in bays
and inlets; byssate closely attached
epifaunal.
Localities: Entire.
Occurrence: Common.
Range: North Carolina to West Indies;
Texas; Yucatán; Quintana Roo; Brazilian
coast to Uruguay.
Remarks: Attaches by byssus to jetties and
oyster reefs; often confused with *B.
citrinus*, Röding, 1798, which is larger and
has 4 anterior teeth.

Genus *Ischadium* Jukes-Brown, 1905

Hooked Mussel
Ischadium recurvum (Rafinesque, 1820)

Size: 25.6–63.5 mm.
Color: Purplish gray.
Shape: Oval with strong triangular hook on
anterior end.
Ornament or sculpture: Strong radial,
rounded ribs dividing near ventral margin;
microscopic growth lines cross ribs.
Hinge area: Umbones at end of hook; 3 or
4 small teeth near umbones; ligament
strong, in large groove extending from
umbones to peak of dorsal margin.
Pallial line & interior: Interior shiny
purple, reddish brown, nacreous; pallial
line simple with 1 large posterior muscle
scar.
Habitat: Oyster reef in low-salinity bays;
byssate closely attached epifaunal.
Localities: Entire.
Occurrence: Common.
Range: Cape Code to West Indies; Texas;
Carmen, Campeche, Mexico; Gulf of
Campeche.
Remarks: Lives on low-salinity oyster reefs.

Subfamily CRENELLINAE Adams & Adams, 1857

Genus *Gregariella* Monterosato, 1884

Common Gregariella
Gregariella coralliophaga (Gmelin, 1791)

Size: 17 mm.
Color: Reddish brown; interior iridescent.
Shape: Oval.
Ornament or sculpture: Smooth except for growth lines; posterior dorsal area somewhat keeled.
Hinge area: Weak, tiny denticulations along hinge.
Pallial line & interior: Pallial line simple; inner edges finely serrate.
Habitat: Bores into rock and coral offshore; semi-infaunal.
Localities: Entire.
Occurrence: Fairly common.
Range: Cape Hatteras to Brazil; Gulf of Mexico; Yucatán.
Remarks: Weaves nest of byssal threads; [*Musculus opifex*]; syn. *G. opifex* (Say, 1815).

Genus *Lioberis* Dall, 1898

Say's Chestnut Mussel
Lioberis castaneus (Say, 1822)

Size: 25 mm.
Color: Bluish white.
Shape: Elongate oval, inflated.
Ornament or sculpture: Smooth except for fine, concentric growth lines.
Hinge area: Umbones slightly back from anterior end; no teeth.
Pallial line & interior: Interior smooth, nacreous; no marginal crenulation; pallial line simple.
Habitat: Open-bay margins, inlets, along shore; infaunal.
Localities: Entire.
Occurrence: Uncommon in beach drift.
Range: South Carolina to Florida Keys and West Indies; Texas; Yucatán; Brazil.
Remarks: [*Botula castanea* (Say 1822)]

Genus *Musculus* Röding, 1798
Subgenus *Ryenella* Fleming, 1959

Lateral Musculus
Musculus (Ryenella) lateralis (Say, 1822)

Subfamily LITHOPHAGINAE Adams & Adams, 1857

Genus *Lithophaga* Röding, 1798
Subgenus *Diberus* Dall, 1898

Mahogany Date Mussel
Lithophaga (Diberus) bisulcata
  (Orbigny, 1845)

Size: 25–38 mm.
Color: Mahogany brown.
Shape: Elongate cylindrical, coming to point at one end.
Ornament or sculpture: Weak concentric growth lines; 2 oblique furrows going from dorsal margin to posterior; covered with gray calcareous deposits.
Hinge area: Umbones not terminal; no teeth.
Pallial line & interior: Anterior muscle in front of umbo.
Habitat: In rocks in both shallow and deep water; infaunal.
Localities: Entire?
Occurrence: Common.
Range: Bermuda; North Carolina to Florida; Texas; West Indies; Surinam; Brazil.
Remarks: Crush jetty rock carefully with hammer to recover these borers; their habit of boring into *Crassostrea virginica* may be of concern to persons cultivating oysters commercially.

Size: 10 mm.
Color: Variable: light brown, pink, or greenish; interior iridescent.
Shape: Oblong.
Ornament or sculpture: Concentric growth lines over entire surface; radial ribs on either end leaving disc section with only finer growth lines.
Hinge area: Umbones not terminal; no teeth.
Pallial line & interior: Pallial line simple.
Habitat: Attached to tunicates; semi-infaunal.
Localities: Entire?
Occurrence: Common.
Range: North Carolina to Florida; Texas; Yucatán; Quintana Roo; West Indies; Brazil.
Remarks: Look in colonies of tunicates (sea pork); attached by byssus.

Subgenus *Myoforceps* P. Fischer, 1886

Scissor Date Mussel
Lithophaga (Myoforceps) aristata
(Dillwyn, 1817)

Size: 25–38 mm.
Color: Grayish white.
Shape: Cylindrical with one end pointed.
Ornament or sculpture: Smooth; points at posterior end that cross each other in scissor-fashion formed by calcareous deposit over periostracum.
Hinge area: Umbones not terminal; no teeth.
Pallial line & interior: Interior nacreous.
Habitat: In rocks in both shallow and deep water; infaunal.
Localities: Entire?
Occurrence: Fairly common.
Range: North Carolina to Florida; Texas; Yucatán; West Indies, La Jolla, California, to Peru.
Remarks: Found in same manner as *L. bisulcata*.

Subfamily MODIOLINAE Keen, 1958

Genus *Modiolus* Lamarck, 1799

Tulip Mussel
Modiolus americanus (Leach, 1815)

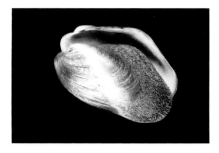

Size: 25–101 mm.
Color: Light brown with blush of rose red and streaks of purple.
Shape: Trigonal.
Ornament or sculpture: Only fine growth lines.
Hinge area: Anterior margin without teeth; umbones away from end of shell; ligament in groove posterior to umbones.
Pallial line & interior: Pallial line weak, simple; posterior muscle scar larger than anterior.
Habitat: Offshore below low-water mark; byssate closely attached epifaunal.
Localities: Entire.
Occurrence: Fairly common beach shell.
Range: Bermuda; North Carolina to West Indies; Texas; Campeche Bank; Yucatán; Surinam; Brazilian coast to Bahia.
Remarks: Color intense red on Texas coast and purple in Florida; [*Volsella* or *Modiolus tulipa* Lamarck, 1819].

Genus *Amygdalum* Megerle von Muhlfeld, 1811

Paper Mussel
Amygdalum papyria (Conrad, 1846)

Size: 25–38 mm.
Color: Exterior grayish; interior iridescent, metallic white.
Shape: Elongate fan-shaped.
Ornament or sculpture: Very delicate and fragile with only fine concentric growth lines.
Hinge area: Umbones slightly beyond anterior end; ligament weak and thin; no teeth.

Pallial line & interior: Pallial line simple and muscle scar faint.
Habitat: Open bays and inlet-influenced areas; semi-infaunal.
Localities: Entire.
Occurrence: Fairly common.
Range: Maryland to Florida; Texas.
Remarks: Carefully dig for these nestlers around roots of marine grass.

Genus *Geukensia* Poel, 1959

Ribbed Mussel
Geukensia demissa granosissima (G. B. Sowerby III, 1914)

Size: 50.8–101 mm.
Color: Brown, shiny.
Shape: Elongate trigonal with rounded posterior margin.
Ornament or sculpture: Numerous strong radial, beaded ribs dividing near posterior margin.
Hinge area: Long, narrow; no teeth; ligament in groove posterior to umbones slightly away from end of shell.
Pallial line & interior: Interior nacreous; pallial line rather strong, simple, with small muscle scar at anterior end and larger one at upper part of posterior end.
Habitat: Salt marshes; byssate closely attached epifaunal.
Localities: Entire.
Occurrence: Common.
Range: Both sides of Florida; Gulf states; Yucatán.
Remarks: Imbeds in roots of marsh grass; referred to as *Modiola demissus* (Dillwyn, 1817).

Superfamily PINNACEA Leach, 1819
Family PINNIDAE Leach, 1819

Genus *Atrina* Gray, 1840

Half-Naked Pen Shell
Atrina seminuda (Lamarck, 1819)

Size: 235–250 mm.
Color: Translucent, grayish tan sometimes mottled with purple brown.
Shape: Wedge-shaped.
Ornament or sculpture: Spinose, radiating ribs with ventral slope usually smooth; ribs often smooth; growth lines fine.
Hinge area: Longest dimension of shell, straight; no teeth.
Pallial line & interior: Nacreous area about one-half to two-thirds length of shell; small posterior adductor muscle scar well within nacreous area, never protruding beyond it; anterior adductor scar small, nearly as wide as anterior end of shell, separates this shell from *A. rigida*; pallial line simple.
Habitat: Offshore and an inlet-influenced bays; semi-infaunal.
Localities: Northwest.
Occurrence: Fairly common.
Range: Eastern United States; Texas; Yucatán; Surinam; Brazil to Argentina.
Remarks: Lives in colonies in mud attached with byssal threads; only posterior margin above substratum; margin of mantle yellow, foot lighter yellow; adductor muscle edible; less common than *A. serrata*; a small crab commensal with and lives within pen shell.

Saw-Tooth Pen Shell
Atrina serrata (G. B. Sowerby I, 1825)

Order PTERIOIDEA Newell, 1965
Suborder PTERIINA Newell, 1965
Superfamily PTERIACEA Gray, 1847
Family PTERIIDAE Gray, 1847

Genus *Pinctada* Röding, 1798
Atlantic Pearl Oyster
Pinctada imbricata Röding, 1798

Size: Up to 250 mm.
Color: Translucent light tan to medium greenish brown.
Shape: Wedge-shaped; thin, fragile, shiny.
Ornament or sculpture: Uniform sculpture of about 30 low ribs covered with fluted projections; sculpture much finer on ventral slope.
Hinge area: Straight to slightly concave without teeth.
Pallial line & interior: Interior has nacreous layer usually covering three-fourths length of valve; posterior adductor muscle scar nearly circular, set well within nacreous layer; anterior scar small; pallial line simple.
Habitat: Offshore in inner shelf zone; semi-infaunal.
Localities: Entire.
Occurrence: Common.
Range: North Carolina to West Indies; Texas; Surinam.
Remarks: Much thinner and spines more tubular than *A. seminuda;* nacreous area larger; at times washed up on outer beaches by hundreds; adductor muscle may be prepared to eat in same way as scallops; harvested in Mexico for canning as scallops; pair of colorless shrimp live commensally with *A. serrata.*

Size: 38–76 mm.
Color: Variable: purplish brown or black.
Shape: Roundish with 2 short wings; inequivalve; inequilateral.
Ornament or sculpture: Flat with concentrically arranged scaly projections of periostracum; byssal gape under anterior wing of right valve.
Hinge area: Straight with single lateral tooth in left valve, double laterals in right.
Pallial line & interior: Interior very nacreous with wide polished border around margins; pallial line simple.
Habitat: Offshore attached to rock or gorgonia, a soft coral; byssate free-swinging epifaunal.
Localities: Entire.
Occurrence: Common.
Range: Southern half of Florida; Texas; Gulf of Mexico to Quintana Roo; West Indies; Brazil.
Remarks: Adults seldom found; forms beautiful pearls; syn. *P. radiata* Leach, 1819

Genus *Pteria* Scopoli, 1777

Atlantic Wing Oyster
Pteria colymbus (Röding, 1798)

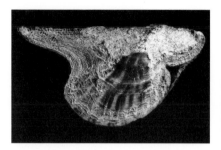

Size: 38–76 mm.
Color: Brownish black with broken, radial lines of cream color; interior highly nacreous.
Shape: Oval with posterior drawn-out wing; inequivalve; inequilateral.
Ornament or sculpture: Smooth surface; byssal gape near anterior wing.
Hinge area: Straight with elongated posterior ear, or wing; 2 small cardinal teeth and 1 lateral tooth in each valve.
Pallial line & interior: Interior nacreous with single, amost central muscle scar; pallial line simple.
Habitat: Offshore reefs; attached to alcyonarians; byssate free-swinging epifaunal.
Localities: Entire?
Occurrence: Common.
Range: Bermuda; southeastern United States; Texas; Costa Rica; West Indies; Brazil.
Remarks: Washes in attached to gorgonia.

Family ISOGNOMONIDAE
  Woodring, 1925

Genus *Isognomon* Lightfoot, 1786

Flat Tree Oyster
Isognomon alatus (Gmelin, 1791)

Size: 50.8–76 mm.
Color: Drab, dirty gray; interior nacreous, purplish.
Shape: Flat, fan-shaped.
Ornament or sculpture: Rough with flaky lamellations.
Hinge area: Straight with 8 to 12 oblong grooves; byssal gape on anterior margin near dorsal margin.
Pallial line & interior: Pallial line simple, discontinuous.
Habitat: In crevices on jetties; byssate free-swinging epifaunal.
Localities: Probably entire.
Occurrence: Fairly common.
Range: Bermuda; southern half of Florida; Texas; southern Mexico; Campeche Bank; Central America; West Indies; Brazilian oceanic islands.
Remarks: Look carefully on mangrove roots. Very undistinguished appearance.

Two-Toned Tree Oyster
Isognomon bicolor (C. B. Adams, 1845)

Superfamily PECTINACEA
  Rafinesque, 1815
  Family PECTINIDAE Rafinesque, 1815
  Subfamily CHLAMYDINAE
    Korobkov, 1960

Genus *Aequipecten* P. Fischer, 1886

Rough Scallop
Aequipecten muscosus (Wood, 1818)

Size: 12–50 mm.
Color: Yellowish with purple splotches; variable.
Shape: Very irregular, elongated parallelogram.
Ornament or sculpture: Rough with flaky lamellations.
Hinge area: Short, straight, with 4 to 8 small, square sockets; anterior byssal gape near dorsal margin.
Pallial line & interior: Sharply raised ridge separates central area from marginal area; color of interior frequently different on opposite sides of ridge; pallial line simple, discontinuous.
Habitat: In clusters on rocks in inlet-influenced areas, byssate free-swinging epifaunal.
Localities: South and Keys.
Occurrence: Uncommon.
Range: Bermuda; Florida Keys; Texas; southern Mexico; Campeche Bank; Yucatán; Costa Rica; Caribbean.
Remarks: More common than *I. alatus.*

Size: 4 cm.
Color: Variable; orange-brown, red, lemon yellow, or mottled with purple.
Shape: Broader than long, left valve convex, right valve flattish. Valves widely gaping.
Ornament or sculpture: 1-20 spinose ribs with 3 rows of spoon-shaped spines; small spines in interspaces.
Hinge area: Ears about same width as shell.
Pallial line & interior: One large muscle scar; pallial line simple.
Habitat: Just offshore on banks; free living, epifaunal.
Localities: West; Keys.
Occurrence: Fairly common.
Range: North Carolina to Florida; Texas to Brazil; Bermuda.

Remarks: The rarer lemon yellow color is much sought after by collectors. Most scales worn off of beach specimens. Trawl for this one.

Genus *Argopectin* Monterosato, 1899

Calico Scallop
Argopectin gibbus (Linné, 1758)

Atlantic Bay Scallop
Argopectin irradians (Lamarck, 1810)

Size: 4 cm.
Color: Upper valve mottled with red or purple. Lower valve white with little color.
Shape: Almost circular.
Ornament or sculpture: About 20 squared ribs. Valves inflated.
Hinge area: Straight, no teeth.
Pallial line & interior: Single muscle scar; pallial line simple.
Habitat: Offshore on intermediate shelf. Free-living epifaunal on sandy and calcareous algae bottoms.
Localities: Entire.
Occurrence: Uncommon.
Range: Maryland to Florida; West Indies; Texas to Brazil; Bermuda.
Remarks: Original name *Ostrea gibba* Linné, 1758. Over-collecting by east coast scallop trawlers is endangering scallop beds.

Size: 5–7.5 cm.
Color: Dull brown or gray, sometimes with yellow. Lower valve is lighter color.
Shape: Both valves convex, not gaping.
Ornament or sculpture: Radial ribs strong and squarish.
Hinge area: Ears about equal in length.
Pallial line & interior: Pallial line simple with single large muscle scar.
Habitat: Semienclosed bays on sand bottoms usually near marine grass.
Localities: Northeast and Northwest.
Occurrence: Common.
Range: Nova Scotia to northern half of Florida and Texas.
Remarks: Young attach by byssal thread. Edible. Best time to collect is mid to late summer.

Genus *Lyropecten* Conrad, 1862
Subgenus *Nodipecten* Dall, 1898

Lion's Paw
Lyropecten (Nodipecten) nodosus
(Linné, 1758)

Subfamily PECTININAE Rafinesque, 1815

Genus *Pecten* Müller, 1776
Subgenus *Euvola* Dall, 1898

Ravenel's Scallop
Pecten (Euvola) raveneli Dall, 1898 [See *SST*, p. 203]

Family PLICATULIDAE Watson, 1930

Genus *Plicatula* Lamarck, 1801

Kitten's Paw
Plicatula gibbosa Lamarck, 1801

Size: 76–152 mm.
Color: Bright red, deep orange, or maroon red.
Shape: Fan-shaped; nearly equivalve; inequilateral.
Ornament or sculpture: 7 to 9 large, coarse ribs that have large, hollow nodules; also numerous cordlike riblets.
Hinge area: Straight; no teeth.
Pallial line & interior: Pallial line simple with single large muscle scar.
Habitat: Offshore; epifaunal fissue dweller.
Localities: Southeastern, south; Keys.
Occurrence: Fairly common.
Range: Florida Keys; Texas; Mexico; West Indies; Surinam; Brazil.
Remarks: Halves of shell found, rarely, on southern part of coast; living speciments found by divers on 7½ Fathon Reef and other offshore banks.

Size: 25 mm.
Color: Whitish with red brown lines on ribs.
Shape: Fan-shaped; inequivalve.
Ornament or sculpture: Rather heavy with 5 to 7 raised ribs that crenulate margin so that valves interlock; attached by right valve.
Hinge area: 2 hinge teeth in each valve lock into corresponding notches in opposite valve, as in *Spondylus;* ligament internal.
Pallial line & interior: Pallial line simple.
Habitat: Offshore on banks; cemented epifaunal.
Localities: Entire.
Occurrence: Common.
Range: Bermuda; North Carolina to Florida; Gulf state; Campeche Bank; Yucatán; West Indies; Surinam; Brazil; Uruguay.
Remarks: Dead shells not uncommon on outer beaches and in spoil banks; look for it attached to pieces of offshore debris

occasionally brought in; attaches by right valve.

Family SPONDYLIDAE Gray, 1826

Genus *Spondylus* Linné, 1758
Atlantic Thorny Oyster
Spondylus americanus Hermann, 1781

(beachworm *Spondylus*)

Size: 76–101 mm.
Color: Variable: white with orange or yellow umbones, rose or cream.
Shape: Nearly circular to oval; inequivalve.
Ornament or sculpture: Adults have spines up to 2 inches in length that are erect, arranged radially; lower valve larger and deeper than upper.
Hinge area: 2 large cardinal teeth on either side of ligament in each valve align with sockets in opposite valve.

Pallial line & interior: Interior smooth and white with 1 large muscle scar; pallial line simple.
Habitat: Offshore attached to reefs; cemented epifaunal.
Localities: Entire.
Occurrence: Uncommon.
Range: North Carolina to Florida; Texas; Campeche Bank; Yucatán; Central America; West Indies; Brazil.
Remarks: Worn, faded valves found on some beaches bear little resemblance to spectacular living specimen brought up by divers offshore; ball-and-socket hinge distinguishes these eroded specimens from *Chama*.

Superfamily ANOMIACEA Rafinesque, 1815
Family ANOMIIDAE Rafinesque, 1815

Genus *Anomia* Linné, 1758
Common Jingle Shell
Anomia simplex Orbigny, 1845

Size: 25–51 mm.
Color: Variable: translucent yellow or dull orange; shiny.
Shape: Subcircular; upper valve more convex than flat attached valve.
Ornament or sculpture: Wavy undulating sculpture; shape conforms to contours and texture of surface on which attached; lower valve has hole near umbones from which chitinous byssus projects to anchor shell.
Hinge area: Ligament not supported with teeth or ridges.
Pallial line & interior: Interior nacreous; pallial line simple, not distinct; upper valve

has large muscle scar opposite hole and 2 smaller ones below.

Habitat: Hypersaline oyster or rock reef; byssate closely attached epifaunal.

Localities: Entire.

Occurrence: Common.

Range: Bermuda; eastern United States; Gulf of Mexico; Gulf of Campeche; Quintana Roo; West Indies to Brazil; Surinam.

Remarks: Often attached to oyster or old shell; usually only top valve found in drift; some old specimens have turned black.

Genus *Pododesmus* Philippi, 1837

Rough Jingle Shell
Pododesmus rudis (Broderip, 1834)

Size: Up to 51 mm.

Color: Brownish; lower valve white.

Shape: Irregular; upper valve convex; lower valve flat with hole near umbones.

Ornament or sculpture: Rough, wavy surface arranged somewhat concentrically.

Hinge area: Narrow; no teeth.

Pallial line & interior: Muscle scar in top valve opposite hole with second large scar diagonally below it; pallial line simple.

Habitat: On rock in inlet-influenced areas; byssate closely attached epifaunal.

Localities: South.

Occurrence: Uncommon.

Range: Bermuda; South Carolina to Florida; Texas; Brazilian coast to Argentina.

Remarks: Syn. *P. decipiens* Philippi, 1837.

Superfamily LIMACEA Rafinesque, 1815
Family LIMIDAE Rafinesque, 1815

Genus *Lima* Bruguière, 1797
Subgenus *Lima* s.s.

Spiny Lima
Lima (Lima) lima (Linné, 1758)

Size: 2.5–3.1 cm.

Color: White.

Shape: Oblique oval, elongate.

Ornament or sculpture: Fragile shell. Radial ribs spinose.

Hinge area: Oblique. Anterior ear much smaller than posterior ear.

Pallial line & interior: Interior polished. Pallial line simple; single muscle scar.

Habitat: Offshore. Epifaunal bysate fissure dweller.
Localities: Southeast.
Occurrence: Fairly common.
Range: Southeastern Florida; southern Texas; Campeche bank; Yucatán; Bermuda; West Indies Brazil; Brazilian oceanic islands.
Remarks: This is a tropical species that occasionally comes to shore attached to bamboo roots or coconuts.

Subgenus *Limaria* Link, 1807

Antillean Lima
Lima (Limaria) pellucida C. B. Adams, 1846 [See *SST*, p. 206]

Suborder OSTREINA Férussac, 1822
Superfamily OSTREACEA Rafinesque, 1815
Family OSTREIDAE Rafinesque, 1815

Genus *Crassostrea* Sacco, 1897

Eastern Oyster
Crassostrea virginica (Gmelin, 1791)

Size: 51–150 mm.
Color: Dull gray.
Shape: Very irregular and variable from oval to weirdly elongate.
Ornament or sculpture: Surface rough with leaflike scales; valve margins slightly undulating or straight; beaks long, curved;

upper valve smaller, flatter, smoother than lower.
Hinge area: Shell attached at umbo of left valve, which is longer than that of right valve; both umbones have central channel for ligamentary attachment.
Pallial line & interior: Muscle scar subcentral, colored deep purple; interior smooth; pallial line simple.
Habitat: Brackish bays and estauries; cemented epifaunal.
Localities: Entire.
Occurrence: Common.
Range: Gulf of St. Lawrence to Gulf of Mexico: Yucatán; West Indies.
Remarks: This commercially important bivalve discussed in Bulletin No. 40 of Texas Game and Fish Commission; does not have interior marginal teeth of *Ostrea equestris*.

Genu *Ostrea* Linné, 1758

Horse or Crested Oyster
Ostrea equestris Say, 1834

Size: 25–51 mm.
Color: Dull gray to brownish; interior gray green.
Shape: Rather oval, fairly constant shape.
Ornament or sculpture: Surface rough with raised, crenulated margins; left valve flatter than right; 6 to 12 teeth on larger valve with corresponding cavities on smaller valve.
Hinge area: Narrow, curved.

Pallial line & interior: Muscle centrally located; scar not pigmented; pallial line simple.
Habitat: High-salinity oyster reef; cemented epifaunal.
Localities: Entire.
Occurrence: Fairly common.
Range: Southeastern United States; Gulf states; West Indies; Brazilian coast to Argentina.
Remarks: Economically important bivalve; requires more saline environment than *Crassostrea virginica* and will replace latter during sustained drought.

Subclass HETERODONTA Neumayr, 1884
Order VENEROIDEA H. & A.
  Adams, 1858
Suborder LUCININA Dall, 1889
Superfamily LUCINACEA Fleming, 1828
Family LUCINIDAE Fleming, 1828
Subfamily LUCININAE Fleming, 1828

Genus *Lucina* Bruguière, 1797
Thick Lucina
Lucina pectinata (Gmelin, 1791)

Size: 25–63 mm.
Color: Pale yellow to orange.
Shape: Oval, lenticular.
Ornament or sculpture: Posterior dorsal slope rostrate, anterior slope less rostrate; sculpture of unequally spaced lamellate ridges with finer lines in interspaces.

Hinge area: Ligament partially visible from outside; lunule small; anterior and posterior lateral teeth strong; cardinals weak.
Pallial line & interior: Pallial line simple with 2 muscle scars; anterior scar very elongate.
Habitat: In grass flats in open-bay margins and hypersaline lagoons; infaunal.
Localities: West.
Occurrence: Fairly common.
Range: North Carolina to Florida; Texas; Quintana Roo; West Indies; Central America to Brazil.
Remarks: [*Phacoides pectinatus*].

Genus *Codakia* Scopoli, 1777
Subgenus *Codakia* s.s.

Tiger Lucina
Codakia (Codakia) orbicularis
  (Linné, 1758)

Size: 63–87 mm.
Color: White.
Shape: Orbicular, compressed; equivalve.
Ornament or sculpture: Reticulate sculpture of coarse radial lines crossed by finer concentric threads.
Hinge area: Lunule in front of beaks deep, heart-shaped, and nearly all on right valve; right valve has 2 cardinal teeth and 1 anterior lateral close to them; left valve has 2 cardinals, large double anterior lateral, and small double posterior lateral.
Pallial line & interior: Pallial line simple with 2 muscle scars.

Habitat: Shallow interreef flats in sand; infaunal.
Localities: Southeast.
Occurrence: Common.
Range: Bermuda; Florida; Texas; Campeche Bank; Yucatán; Costa Rica; northeastern and eastern Brazil.
Remarks: *Codakia obiculata* (Montagu, 1808) is a different species.

Genus *Linga* De Gregorio, 1884
Subgenus *Bellucina* Dall, 1901

Lovely Miniature Lucina
[*Linga (Bellucina) amianta* (Dall, 1901)]

Size: 6–10 mm.
Color: White.
Shape: Orbicular; equivalve; subequilateral.
Ornament or sculpture: Rather inflated, thickened shell; sculptured with 8 to 9 wide, rounded ribs crossed by numerous, small concentric threads.
Hinge area: Umbones touching; lunule small; cardinal teeth small, not visible in adults; laterals well developed in right valve with sockets in left.
Pallial line & interior: Pallial line simple with 2 muscle scars; margin crenulate.

Habitat: Inlet-influenced areas and near shore; infaunal.
Localities: Entire.
Occurrence: Common in beach drift.
Range: North Carolina to both sides of Florida; Texas; northeastern and eastern Brazil.
Remarks: Panamic vicariant is *L. cancellaris* Philippi, 1846. [*Lucina amiantus*].

Genus *Parvilucina* Dall, 1901

Many-Lined Lucina
Parvilucina multilineata (Holmes, 1859)

Size: 6–10 mm.
Color: White.
Shape: Orbicular; equivalve.
Ornament or sculpture: Sculpture of numerous, fine, concentric threads stronger near umbones.
Hinge area: Small cardinal and lateral teeth in right and left valves; umbones small.
Pallial line & interior: Pallial line simple with 2 muscle scars; interior margin finely crenulate.
Habitat: Offshore and inlet-influenced areas; infaunal.
Localities: Entire.
Occurrence: Common in beach drift.

Range: North Carolina to both sides of Florida; Texas; Yucatán; Quintana Roo; eastern and southern Brazil.
Remarks: More common to south; [*Lucina multilineata*]; syn. *Linga crenella* Dall, 1901.

Subfamily MILTHINAE Chavan, 1969

Genus *Anodontia* Link, 1807
Buttercup Lucina
Anodontia alba Link, 1807

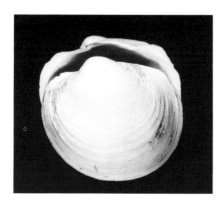

Size: 38–51 mm.
Color: Exterior white; interior flushed with yellowish orange.
Shape: Oval or circular, inflated; equivalve.
Ornament or sculpture: Sculpture of weak, irregular concentric growth lines.
Hinge area: Hinge with weak teeth; umbones not prominent; hinge extended anteriorly to faint oval lunule.
Pallial line & interior: Pallial line simple with 2 muscle scars; anterior scar elongate, nearly parallel to pallial line; margins smooth.
Habitat: Inlet-influenced areas, bay margins, hypersaline lagoons; infaunal.
Localities: Entire.
Occurrence: Fairly common beach shell.
Range: Bermuda; North Carolina to Florida; Gulf states; Campeche Bank; Yucatán; Costa Rica; West Indies.
Remarks: Likes sandy bottoms. Syn. *Lucina chrysostoma* Philippi, 1847.

Chalky Buttercup
Anodontia philippiana (Reeve, 1850)

Size: 51–101 mm.
Color: Chalky white.
Shape: Orbicular, inflated; equivalve.
Ornament or sculpture: Fine concentric growth lines; interior usually pustulose.
Hinge area: Umbones rounded and touching; hinge with very weak teeth.
Pallial line & interior: Pallial line simple with 2 muscle scars; anterior scar juts away from line at 30° angle instead of being parallel as in *A. alba*.
Habitat: Offshore at moderate depths; infaunal.
Localities: Southeast.
Occurrence: Uncommon beach shell.
Range: Bermuda; North Carolina to eastern Florida; Texas; Cuba.
Remarks: May be same as *A. schrammi* (Crosse, 1876).

Genus *Pseudomiltha* P. Fischer, 1885

Florida Lucina
Pseudomiltha floridana (Conrad, 1833)

Family UNGULINIDAE
H. & A. Adams, 1857

Genus *Diplodonta* Bronn, 1831
Subgenus *Phlyctiderma* Dall, 1899

Pimpled Diplodon
Diplodonta (Phlyctiderma) semiaspera
   Philippi, 1836

Size: 3.8 mm.
Color: White.
Shape: Orbicular; equivalve; subequilateral.
Ornament or sculpture: Compressed; rather smooth except for fine, irregular growth lines.
Hinge area: Umbones low and pointing forward; lunule oval; hinge margin thick but teeth weakly defined.
Pallial line & interior: Pallial line simple with 2 muscle scars; anterior scar elongate.
Habitat: Open bays and inlet-influenced areas; infaunal.
Localities: West.
Occurrence: Fairly common.
Range: Western coast of Florida to Texas.
Remarks: Some writers place in genus *Megaxinus* Brugnone, 1880; [*Lucina floridana*].

Size: Up to 12 mm.
Color: Chalky white.
Shape: Orbicular, inflated; equivalve.
Ornament or sculpture: Thin shell marked with numerous concentric rows of microscopic pimples.
Hinge area: Two cardinal teeth in each valve; laterals absent; left anterior and right posterior ones split.
Pallial line & interior: Pallial line simple with 2 elongate muscle scars.

Habitat: Open-bay centers, jetties, inlet-influenced areas; infaunal.
Localities: Entire.
Occurrence: Fairly common.
Range: North Carolina to Florida; Texas; Yucatán; West Indies; Brazilian coast to Uruguay.
Remarks: Found by breaking jetty rocks, also in old *Crassostrea* and *Mercenaria* shells; builds nests around itself of mud and sand held together with mucus; does not appear to be equipped to bore.

Order HIPPURITOIDEA Newell, 1965 = [PACHYDONTA Steinman, 1903]
Superfamily CHAMACEA Blainville, 1825
Family CHAMIDAE Lamarck, 1809

Genus *Chama* Linné, 1758

Little Corrugated Jewel Box
Chama congregata Conrad, 1833

Size: Up to 25 mm.
Color: Red.
Shape: Round; right, or upper, valve much smaller than left.
Ornament or sculpture: Surface covered with numerous low axial corrugations; left valve attached; umbones twist to right; never has foliaceous appearance of *C. macerophylla*.
Hinge area: Umbones turn from right to left; 2 cardinal teeth, 1 heavy and rough in left valve, 2 widely separated small teeth in right; both valves with 1 small posterior lateral tooth.
Pallial line & interior: Pallial line simple, connecting 2 muscle scars.
Habitat: Offshore on calcareous banks; cemented epifaunal.
Localities: Entire.
Occurrence: Uncommon beach shell.
Range: North Carolina to Florida; Texas; West Indies; Central America.
Remarks: Usually only badly eroded right valves found in drift; shell often found attached to valves of *Atrina serrata* (Sowerby, 1815).

Leafy Jewel Box
Chama macerophylla (Gmelin, 1791) [See SST, p. 213]

Genus *Pseudochama* Odhner, 1917

Atlantic Left-Handed Jewel Box
Pseudochama radians (Lamarck, 1819) [See SST, p. 213]

Genus *Arcinella* Schumacher, 1817

True Spiny Jewel Box
Arcinella cornuta Conrad, 1866

Size: 25–38 mm.
Color: White.
Shape: Quadrate, inflated.

Ornament or sculpture: 7 to 9 radial rows of heavy, short spines; heavy shell; coarse granulations between ribs.
Hinge area: Umbones curved forward over large, wide, heart-shaped lunule; large cardinal tooth in left valve.
Pallial line & interior: Pallial line smple, connecting 2 muscle scars.
Habitat: Offshore on calcareous banks; cemented epifaunal.
Localities: Entire, more to south.
Occurrence: Fairly common on beach.
Range: North Carolina; Florida; Texas to Carmen, Campeche, Mexico; Yucatán.
Remarks: Begins and ends life free swimming (attached by right valve in interim); [*Echinochama cornuta*].

Superfamily LEPTONACEA Gray, 1847
Family MONTACUTIDAE Clark, 1855

Genus *Mysella* Angas, 1877

Atlantic Flat Lepton
Mysella planulata (Stimpson, 1851)

Size: 3.5 mm.
Color: White.
Shape: Oblong oval, flattened; equivalve; inequilateral.
Ornament or sculpture: Smooth with only fine concentric growth lines.
Hinge area: Small pointed beaks three-fourths of distance back from anterior end; dorsal margin depressed in front and back of beaks.
Pallial line & interior: Pallial line simple with 2 suboval, almost equal muscle scars.
Habitat: Attaches to pilings, buoys, grasses in bays and shallow water; epifaunal.
Localities: Entire.
Occurrence: Fairly common in beach drift.
Range: Greenland to Texas; West Indies.
Remarks: Easily overlooked and confused with *Aligena texasiana*.

Superfamily CARDITACEA Fleming, 1820
Family CARDITIDAE Fleming, 1820
Subfamily CARDITAMERINAE
  Chavan, 1969

Genus *Carditamera* Conrad, 1838

Broad-Ribbed Cardita
Carditamera floridana Conrad, 1838

Size: 25–63 mm.
Color: Whitish, with small bars of chestnut brown arranged concentrically on ribs.
Shape: Oval; equivalve; inequilateral.
Ornament or sculpture: 15 to 18 strong radiating ribs, beaded by transverse growth lines; beaks close together.
Hinge area: External hinge ligament; hinge oblique; strong cardinal teeth; right valve has 1 anterior lateral, left valve 1 posterior

lateral tooth; lunule small, deeply indented under beaks.
Pallial line & interior: Interior smooth with 2 muscle scars.
Habitat: Inlet-influenced areas and hypersaline lagoons; infaunal.
Localities: Southern half of coast.
Occurrence: Common beach shell.
Range: Southern half of Florida; southern Texas to Mexico; Gulf of Campeche; Yucatán; Quintana Roo.
Remarks: Attaches by byssus [*Cardita floridana*].

Superfamily CRASSATELLACEA
    Férussac, 1821
Family CRASSATELLIDAE Férussac, 1821
Subfamily SCAMBULINAE Chavan, 1852

Genus *Crassinella* Guppy, 1874

Lunate Crasinella
Crassinella lunulata (Conrad, 1834)

Size: 6–8 mm.
Color: Whitish or pinkish; interior brown; very colorful.
Shape: Trigonal; slightly inequivalve.
Ornament or sculpture: Beaks at middle; valves lapped so posterior dorsal margin of left valve more visible than right; flattened valves sculptured with well-developed concentric ribs and microscopic articulation.
Hinge area: Ligament internal; 2 cardinal teeth on each side, 1 anterior lateral in right, 1 posterior in left.
Pallial line & interior: Pallial line simple, joining 2 adductor muscle scars.
Habitat: Inlet-influenced areas and channels on shelly bottom; infaunal.
Localities: Entire.
Occurrence: Fairly common.
Range: Bermuda; Cape Cod south to Florida; northern Gulf of Mexico; Yucatán; Quintana Roo; West Indies; northern and northeastern Brazil.
Remarks: Syn. *C. quadelupensis* Orbigny, 1846.

Superfamily CARDIACEA Lamarck, 1809
Family CARDIIDAE Lamarck, 1809
Subfamily TRACHYCARDIINAE
    Stewart, 1930

Genus *Trachycardium* Mörch, 1853
Subgenus *Dallocardia* Stewart, 1930

Yellow Cockle
Trachycardium (Dallocardia) muricatum
    (Linné, 1758)

Size: 51 mm.
Color: Light cream with blotches of red brown or shades of yellow; interior white.
Shape: Subcircular, inflated; equivalve.
Ornament or sculpture: 30 to 40 sharply scaled ribs; scales on anterior slope on anterior side of ribs, while on central and posterior slopes on posterior side of ribs; separation marked by several ribs with double rows of spines.
Hinge area: Umbones prominent, nearly central; ligament external; cardinal and lateral teeth present.
Pallial line & interior: Interior margin crenate; pallial line indistinct, simple, connecting 2 equal-sized adductor muscle scars.
Habitat: Inlet-influenced areas and bay margins; infaunal.
Localities: Entire.
Occurrence: Fairly common.
Range: North Carolina to Florida; Texas; Carmen, Campeche, Mexico; Gulf of Campeche; Yucatán; West Indies; Surinam; Brazil to Uruguay.
Remarks: After sustained freeze will pop out of sandy mud along lower bay margins; double siphons short, and foot well developed for digging.

Subfamily LAEVICARDIINAE Keen, 1936

Genus *Laevicardium* Swainson, 1840

Common Egg Cockle
Laevicardium laevigatum (Linné, 1758)

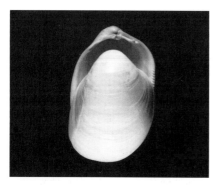

Size: 25–51 mm.
Color: Cream colored or pale yellow variably mottled with brown.
Shape: Obliquely egg-shaped.
Ornament or sculpture: Smooth, polished with obscure radiating ribs.
Hinge area: Umbones rounded; cardinal and lateral teeth present.
Pallial line & interior: Interior cream colored with finely serrated margins; pallial line simple, connecting 2 muscle scars; ventral margin crenulate.
Habitat: Offshore; infaunal.
Localities: Entire.
Occurrence: Common.
Range: Bermuda; North Carolina to both sides of Florida; Texas; Campeche Bank; Yucatán; Central America; West Indies; Surinam; Brazil.
Remarks: Beach shells are bleached white.

Morton's Egg Cockle
Laevicardium mortoni (Conrad, 1830)

Size: 16–25 mm.
Color: Exterior cream colored, irregularly patterned with brown; interior yellow with brown mottlings.
Shape: Oval, inflated; equivalve.
Ornament or sculpture: Smooth, polished, with faint concentric lines microscopically pimpled; shell thin.
Hinge area: Cardinal and lateral teeth present; anterior laterals prominent.

Pallial line & interior: Pallial line simple, connecting 2 muscle scars; margins may or may not be crenulated.
Habitat: Shallow water in inlet-influenced areas and hypersaline lagoons; infaunal.
Localities: Entire, except for west coast.
Occurrence: Common.
Range: Cape Cod to Florida; Texas to Tecolutla, Mexico; Yucatán; Quintana Roo; West Indies.
Remarks: Can swim and hop about in shallow waters with surprising speed. Ducks love it.

Subgenus *Dinocardium* Dall, 1900

Giant Atlantic Cockle
Laevicardium (Dinocardium) robustum (Lightfoot, 1786)

Size: 76–101 mm.
Color: Pale tan, mottled with red brown; posterior slope mahogany brown; interior salmon pink.
Shape: Obliquely ovate, inflated; equivalve.
Ornament or sculpture: 32 to 36 rounded, radial smoothish ribs.
Hinge area: Umbones rounded; heavy external ligament; 1 cardinal tooth in each valve, with 2 anterior lateral and 1 posterior lateral in right valve; complementary arrangement in left valve.
Pallial line & interior: Pallial line simple, connecting 2 muscle scars; margins crenulate.

Habitat: Close to shore and in inlet-influenced areas; infaunal.
Localities: Entire, except for southwest coast.
Occurrence: Common.
Range: Virginia to northern Florida; Texas; Carmen, Campeche, Mexico.
Remarks: Largest cockle on Florida coast; storms often wash great numbers in alive. On west coast the most common large cockle is the more colorful, elongate *Dinocardium robustum vanhyningi* Clench & L.C. Smith, 1944, a more narrow and colorful species.

Superfamily MACTRACEA Lamarck, 1809
Family MACTRIDAE Lamarck, 1809
Subfamily MACTRINAE Lamarck, 1809

Genus *Mactra* Linné, 1767

Fragile Atlantic Mactra
Mactra fragilis Gmelin, 1791

Size: 38–63 mm.
Color: White.
Shape: Oval; equivalve; subequilateral.
Ornament or sculpture: Margins rounded; sculpture of fine, irregular growth lines; posterior slope with 2 radial ridges; fairly large posterior gape.
Hinge area: Umbones rounded, almost central; 2 ligaments, 1 external, inner cartilaginous ligament housed in spoon-shaped chondrophore posterior to bifid cardinal tooth.
Pallial line & interior: Polished white interior with lightly impressed scars of

about equal size and shape; pallial sinus short, broadly rounded.
Habitat: Open-bay margins; infaunal.
Localities: Entire.
Occurrence: Fairly common.
Range: North Carolina to Florida; Texas; West Indies; Surinam.
Remarks: Syn. *M. brasiliana* Lamarck, 1818.

Genus *Mulinia* Gray, 1837
Dwarf Surf Clam
Mulinia lateralis (Say, 1822)

Size: 8–16 mm.
Color: Whitish to cream.
Shape: Trigonal, inflated; inequilateral.
Ornament or sculpture: Smooth except for fine growth lines; posterior slope marked with distinct radial ridge.
Hinge area: Umbones high, almost central; chondrophore, bifid cardinals, lateral teeth make up hinge complex.
Pallial line & interior: Anterior adductor scar more elongate than posterior scar; pallial sinus short, rounded, oblique.
Habitat: Clayey sediments in every type of assemblage; infaunal.
Localities: Northwest.
Occurrence: Very common.
Range: Maine to northern Florida; Texas; Gulf of Campeche; Yucatán.
Remarks: Can withstand wide range of salinities; juveniles thin and opalescent, coming to shore in vast numbers in winter months.

Genus *Rangia* Des Moulins, 1832
Subgenus *Rangia* s.s.
Common Rangia
Rangia (Rangia) cuneata (Gray, 1831)

Size: 25–80 mm.
Color: Whitish.
Shape: Obliquely ovate; equivalve; inequilateral.
Ornament or sculpture: Heavy, thick shell sculptured with fine concentric growth lines.
Hinge area: Deeply excavated chondrophore, cardinals, 2 lateral teeth; posterior lateral very long, reaching almost to ventral margin, easily separating it from *R. flexuosa*; umbones prominent, nearer anterior end.
Pallial line & interior: Anterior adductor scar smaller than posterior scar; pallial sinus small but distinct, directed forward and upward.
Habitat: River-influenced areas; infaunal.
Localities: Northwest.
Occurrence: Common.
Range: New Jersey; northwestern Florida to Texas and to Alvarado, Veracruz, Mexico.
Remarks: A brackish-water species; recent studies indicate that suspended solids in water above substratum where *Rangia* live significantly inhibit their growth more than do characteristics of substratum itself.

Genus *Spisula* Gray, 1837
Subgenus *Hemimactra* Swainson, 1840

Atlantic Surf Clam
Spisula (Hemimactra) solidissima similis
(Say, 1822)

Subfamily PTEROPSELLINAE Keen, 1969

Genus *Anatina* Schumacher, 1817

Smooth Duck Clam
Anatina anatina (Spengler, 1802)

Size: 101–127 mm.
Color: Yellowish white.
Shape: Oval.
Ornament or sculpture: Smooth except for fine, concentric growth lines.
Hinge area: Large, shallow, triangular umbones acute, more anteriorly located; chondrophore; 2 cardinal teeth, those in left valve fused at upper ends; opposite deep socket in lateral teeth.
Pallial line & interior: Adductor muscle scars rounded, above middle of valve; pallial sinus short, rounded, almost parallel to pallial line.
Habitat: Inlet-influenced areas; infaunal.
Localities: Entire.
Occurrence: Fairly common beach shell.
Range: Cape Cod; both sides of Florida; Texas.
Remarks: Edible bivalve but not in commercial quantities; syn. *S. s. raveneli* (Conrad, 1831).

Size: 50–76 mm.
Color: White.
Shape: Trigonal; inequilateral.
Ornament or sculpture: Thin, fragile, gaping posteriorly; fairly smooth, except for fine growth lines and concentric ribs near umbones; distinct radial rib on posterior end.
Hinge area: Prominent chondrophore and 3 small cardinal teeth anterior to chondrophore; lateral tooth posterior to chondrophore; umbones high, pointed backward.
Pallial line & interior: Anterior adductor scar elongate; posterior scar rounded; pallial sinus narrow, deep.
Habitat: Surf zone to 40 fathoms; infaunal.
Localities: Entire.
Occurrence: Uncommon beach shell.
Range: North Carolina to northern two-thirds of Florida; Texas; Mexico; Puerto Rico; Brazil.
Remarks: Seldom found except in winter less common than *Raeta plicatella*; syn. *Labiosa lineata* (Say, 1822).

Genus *Raeta* Gray, 1853
Channeled Duck Clam
Raeta plicatella (Lamarck, 1818)

Family MESODESMATIDAE Gray, 1839
Subfamily ERVILIINAE Dall, 1895

Genus *Ervilia* Turton, 1822
Ervilia cf. *E. concentrica* (Holmes, 1860)

Size: 50–76 mm.
Color: White.
Shape: Trigonal; inequilateral.
Ornament or sculpture: Thin, fragile, gaping posteriorly; sculpture of evenly spaced, rounded concentric ribs with fine striations in intercostal spaces; fine radial threads.
Hinge area: Prominent chondrophore; small, irregular cardinal teeth; single lateral tooth posterior to chondrophore; umbones high, pointed backward.
Pallial line & interior: Anterior adductor scar elongate; posterior scar to about midshell almost parallel to pallial line, somewhat pointed.
Habitat: Probably does not burrow but lives on side on sandy bottom of outer surf zone; epifaunal.
Localities: Entire.
Occurrence: Fairly common.
Range: North Carolina to Florida; Texas; Mexico; West Indies; Surinam; Brazil to Argentina.
Remarks: More common on beaches in winter; syn. *Anatina canaliculata* (Say, 1822).

Size: 5–6 mm.
Color: White.
Shape: Elliptical; equilateral.
Ornament or sculpture: Sculpture of fine, numerous concentric lines; quite variable.
Hinge area: Umbones central; resilium small, internal; cardinal tooth bifid; laterals small.
Pallial line & interior: Muscle scars faintly impressed; pallial sinus rounded, broad, short.
Habitat: Near shore; infaunal.
Localities: Entire, more to south.
Occurrence: Fairly common in beach drift.
Range: Bermuda; North Carolina to both sides of Florida; Texas; Quintana Roo; West Indies to Brazil.
Remarks: Because of similarity to juvenile *Mulinias,* may be overlooked.

Superfamily SOLENACEA Lamarck, 1809
Family SOLENIDAE Lamarck, 1809

Genus *Solen* Linné, 1758

Green Jackknife Clam
Solen viridis Say, 1822

Family CULTELLIDAE Davis, 1935

Genus *Ensis* Schumacher, 1817

Jackknife Clam
Ensis minor Dall, 1900

Size: Up to 51 mm.
Color: White.
Shape: Long, narrow, flattened cylindrical; equivalve.
Ornament or sculpture: Dorsal edge straight; ventral edge curved; fragile.
Hinge area: Single projecting tooth at very end of valve.
Pallial line & interior: Pallial line has 2 muscle scars and pallial sinus.
Habitat: Inlets, near shore; infaunal.
Localities: Northwest.
Occurrence: Fairly common.
Range: Rhode Island to northern Florida; Gulf states.
Remarks: Easily confused with *Ensis minor* but much shorter; figure that of juvenile.

Size: Up to 76 mm.
Color: Shell white; interior purplish.
Shape: Cylindrical; equivalve.
Ornament or sculpture: Long narrow shell smooth, fragile.
Hinge area: Left valve has 2 vertical cardinal teeth; each valve has long low posterior tooth; teeth in less pointed end.
Pallial line & interior: 2 adductor muscle scars; pallial sinus shallow.
Habitat: Enclosed lagoon and bay margins; infaunal.
Localities: South through northwest.
Occurrence: Fairly common.
Range: New Jersey to Florida to Texas.
Remarks: A favorite food of wading birds.

Superfamily TELLINACEA Blainville, 1824
Family TELLINIDAE Blainville, 1824
Subfamily TELLININAE Blainville, 1824

Genus *Tellina* Linné, 1758
Subgenus *Tellina* Linné, 1758

Sunrise Tellin
Tellina radiata Linné, 1758

Subgenus *Angulus* Megerle von Mühlfeld, 1811

Tampa Tellin
Tellina (Angulus) tampaensis
Conrad, 1866

Size: 5–10 cm.
Color: Cream rayed with light red or yellow. Interior yellow.
Shape: Elongate, moderately inflated.
Ornament or sculpture: Smooth, highly polished surface.
Hinge area: 2 cardinal and 2 lateral teeth in each valve. Beaks tipped with red.
Pallial line & interior: Pallial sinus touches the anterior muscle scar.
Habitat: Offshore coral sand in shallow water.
Localities: South.
Occurrence: Common.
Range: North Carolina to southern half of Florida and West Indies; Bermuda.
Remarks: A favorite of collectors.

Size: 13–24 mm.
Color: Smooth white, frequently suffused with pale peach coloration; interior polished.
Shape: Ovate subtrigonal; inequivalve; inequilateral.
Ornament or sculpture: Anterior margin broadly rounded; posterior dorsal margin steeply sloping; sculpture of concentric lines separated by narrow, well-defined sulci.
Hinge area: Ligament brown, external; cardinal teeth present, but no true lateral teeth produced.
Pallial line & interior: Adductor muscle scars well impressed; anterior scar longer, narrower, higher than posterior scar; pallial sinus descends to pallial line in short, straight drop some distance from anterior scar.
Habitat: Hypersaline lagoons; infaunal.
Localities: South.
Occurrence: Fairly common.
Range: Southern half of Florida to Texas; Bahamas; Cuba.
Remarks: Look along Packery Channel.

Say's Tellin
Tellina (Angulus) texana Dall, 1900

DeKay's Dwarf Tellin
Tellina (Angulus) versicolor DeKay, 1843

Size: 16.5 mm.
Color: White with opalescent interior.
Shape: Subelliptical to subtrigonal; inequivalve; inequilateral.
Ornament or sculpture: Anterior margin rounded; posterior dorsal margin elongate, steeply inclined; sculpture of weak, finely incised, closely spaced concentric sulci.
Hinge area: Ligament yellowish brown, strong, external; cardinal teeth but no true lateral teeth; umbones posterior to middle, blunt.
Pallial line & interior: Adductor muscle scars fairly well impressed; anterior scar elongate, rounded below; posterior scar rounded; pallial sinus convex above, gently inclined and slightly concave anteriorly, falling in arch to pallial line near but not touching anterior scar.
Habitat: Bay centers; infaunal.
Localities: Northwest.
Occurrence: Fairly common.
Range: North Carolina to southern half of Florida; Texas; Cuba.
Remarks: Holotype collected by J. A. Singley at Corpus Christi Bay, Texas, ca. 1893; tolerates lower salinity than many other tellins; syn. *T. sayi* Dall, 1900.

Size: 14 mm.
Color: Translucent with red, white, or pink rays; shiny.
Shape: Elongate, subelliptical.
Ornament or sculpture: Anterior dorsal margin elongate, slightly inclined; posterior dorsal margin steeply inclined, short, slightly concave; posterior marked with rounded keel; sculpture of widely spaced, strongly incised concentric sulci; no radial sculpture.
Hinge area: Umbones just posterior to middle, depressed, pointed; ligament yellowish brown, external; right valve has cardinal teeth and weak laterals; left valve has cardinal teeth but no laterals.
Pallial line & interior: Anterior adductor scar elongate, rounded below; posterior scar rounded; pallial sinus rises gently posteriorly, convex above, arches down to pallial line very near anterior scar, at times touching it.
Habitat: Bays and offshore in sandy mud; infaunal.
Localities: Entire:
Occurrence: Common.
Range: Rhode Island to southern half of Florida; Texas; Campeche Bank; West Indies.
Remarks: Without magnification can be confused with *T. iris* but lacks distinctive oblique sculpture of *T. iris*.

Subgenus *Eurytellina* Fischer, 1887

Alternate Tellin
Tellina (Eurytellina) alternata Say, 1822

Rose Petal Tellin
Tellina (Eurytellina) lineata Turton, 1819

Size: 70 mm.
Color: Glossy white, often with slight blushes of pink or yellow.
Shape: Elongate, subtrigonal; inequivalve; inequilateral.
Ornament or sculpture: Outline narrow posteriorly with slight truncation; sculpture of incised concentric lines separated by broad bands; left valve has broader bands and fewer lines than right; posterior ridge occurs in right valve; every alternate striation disappears at angle of keel.
Hinge area: Umbones slightly posterior to center, small, scarcely elevated; ligament strong, brown, exterior; 3 cardinal teeth in right valve; both valves have internal rib extending from umbo to anterior muscle scar.
Pallial line & interior: Adductor muscle scars well impressed; pallial sinus curves upward toward umbones, extends anteriorly almost to muscle scar.
Habitat: Sand near shore, bay margins, inlets; infaunal.
Localities: South through northwest.
Occurrence: Fairly common.
Range: North Carolina; Florida; Gulf states; Yucatán; Costa Rica; West Indies; southern Brazil.
Remarks: Until recently considered closely related to *T. a. tayloriana*; valves of *T. alternata* somewhat more inflated and less colorful.

Size: 25–34 mm.
Color: Pink to white.
Shape: Elongate subtrigonal; equivalve; inequilateral.
Ornament or sculpture: Anterior margin well rounded; posterior dorsal margin steeply sloping; sculpture of close, weak, concentric sulci separated by low, narrow bands; posterior ridge present but not well developed, stronger on left valve; twist to right at posterior end.
Hinge area: Ligament dark brown, short, wide, sunken; umbones slighty raised, pointed, inflated, located just posterior to middle; both cardinal and lateral teeth present, posterior lateral well developed; variable anterior rib between umbones and anterior scar.
Pallial line & interior: Adductor muscle scars well impressed; pallial sinus convex above, not rising above adductor muscle scars, extending closer to anterior scar than that of *T. alternata tayloriana*.
Habitat: Offshore or dead in spoil banks; infaunal.
Localities: Entire.
Occurrence: Common.
Range: All of Florida; Texas; Yucatán; Costa Rica; West Indies; Brazil.
Remarks: Shape and color variable, but strong twist of valves to right posteriorly and umbones pointing to back are consistent.

Subgenus *Lanciolina* Iredale, 1737
Great Tellin
Tellina magna Spengler, 1798

Size: 7.6–11.30 cm.
Color: Left valve is white; right valve orange to pinkish.
Shape: Quite laterally compressed; posterior more pointed.
Ornament or sculpture: Glossy, smooth, with microscopic concentric lines.
Hinge area: Only right anterior lateral tooth developed. Strong, brown ligament.
Pallial line & interior: Long pallial sinus.
Habitat: Just below low tide in sand.
Localities: Southeast.
Occurrence: Uncommon.
Range: North Carolina to southern half of Florida and West Indies; Bermuda.
Remarks: The largest tellin in Florida.

Subgenus *Tellinella* Mörch, 1853
Speckeled Tellin
Tellina listeri Röding, 1798

Size: 6–8.9 cm.
Color: Whitish with numerous small zig-zagged speckles of purplish-brown. Interior yellowish.
Shape: Elongate, moderately inflated; twisted posteriorly to the right.
Ornament or sculpture: Strong concentric treads.
Hinge area: Right anterior lateral tooth distant from cardinals.
Pallial line & interior: Pallial sinus connected to front muscle scar by a linear scar.
Habitat: Coarse sand in shallow water.
Localities: South.
Occurrence: Fairly common.
Range: North Carolina to southern half of Florida and West Indies; Bermuda; Brazil.
Remarks: Young specimens are longer and rougher.

Subgenus *Merisca* Dall, 1900
Lintea Tellin
Tellina (Merisca) aequistriata (Say, 1824)

Size: 9–24 mm.
Color: White.

Shape: Moderately oval; inequilateral.
Ornament or sculpture: Sculpture of numerous sharp, concentric ridges; left valve has 1 posterior radial ridge, right valve 2; posterior margin narrow, flexed.
Hinge area: Umbones small, sharp; ligament small; weak hinge area has 2 long laterals in left valve.
Pallial line & interior: Muscle scars small; dorsal line of pallial sinus meets pallial line near anterior scar.
Habitat: Offshore in sand, 5 to 15 meters (9 to 28 fathoms); infaunal.
Localities: West.
Occurrence: Uncommon.
Range: North Carolina to Florida; Texas; Campeche Bank; Yucatan; West Indies; Brazilian coast to Bahia.
Remarks: Syn. *Quadrans lintea* Conrad, 1837; distinguished by posterior twist.

Subgenus *Scissula* Dall, 1900
Iris Tellin
Tellina (Scissula) iris Say, 1822

Shape: Elongate, elliptical; equivalve; inequilateral.
Ornament or sculpture: Anterior dorsal margin long, gently sloping to rounded anterior margin; posterior margin obliquely truncated; posterior slope slightly keeled; sculpture of faint growth lines more developed posteriorly, crossed by well-developed, widely spaced oblique lines.
Hinge area: Umbones posterior to middle, small, slightly pointed; ligament light yellow brown, weak, external; left valve has cardinal teeth but no true lateral teeth; right valve has cardinal teeth and interior lateral tooth but no posterior lateral.
Pallial line & interior: Adductor scars weak; anterior scar irregularly quadrate; posterior scar rounded; pallial sinus rises abruptly posteriorly, descends gently, arches to pallial line, well separated from anterior scar.
Habitat: Near shore and inlet areas; infaunal.
Localities: Northwest.
Occurrence: Common.
Range: Bermuda; North Carolina to Florida; Gulf of Mexico.
Remarks: Common in winter beach drift.

Genus *Tellidora* H. & A. Adams, 1856
White Crested Tellin
Tellidora cristata (Récluz, 1842)

Size: 15.3 mm.
Color: Transparent to translucent suffused with pink; 2 white rays often occur in posterior quarter.

Size: Up to 37 mm.
Color: White.

Shape: Subtrigonal, very compressed; inequivalve; inequilateral.

Ornament or sculpture: Anterior and posterior dorsal margins have triangular spines; sculpture of strong, narrow, concentric ridges; spines form deep lunule and escutcheon.

Hinge area: Umbones central, acute, elevated; ligament brown, short, partially internal; 2 cardinal teeth in each valve and strong, triangular, anterior lateral tooth in right valve.

Pallial line & interior: Adductor scars well impressed; anterior scar more elongate than posterior; pallial sinus short, widely separated from anterior scar, arches down to pallial line near posterior end.

Habitat: Inlets and channels; bay margins in sandy bottoms; infaunal.

Localities: Southeast through west.

Occurrence: Uncommon.

Range: North Carolina to western Florida and Texas; Yucatán.

Remarks: Dorsal spines make this clam unique.

Genus *Strigilla* Turton, 1822
Subgenus *Pisostrigilla* Olsson, 1961

White Strigilla
Strigilla (Pisostrigilla) mirabilis
(Philippi, 1841)

Size: 8 mm.
Color: White, translucent, shiny.
Shape: Oval, inflated; inequivalve; equilateral.

Ornament or sculpture: Sculpture of fine growth lines crossed by oblique lines that meet ventral margin at about 45°; posterior slope patterned with 4 or more zigzag rows of lines.

Hinge area: Umbones rounded, almost central; 2 cardinals and 2 lateral teeth present; left posterior cardinal very thin, fragile.

Pallial line & interior: Large pallial sinus runs forward but does not touch anterior muscle scar; weak cruciform muscle scars near ventral margin.

Habitat: Offshore; infaunal.

Localities: Entire.

Occurrence: Uncommon in beach drift.

Range: Bermuda; southeastern United States; Texas; Campeche Bank; West Indies; northeastern Brazil.

Remarks: Oblique sculpture distinctive.

Subfamily MACOMINAE Olsson, 1961

Genus *Macoma* Leach, 1819

Tenta Macoma
Macoma tenta (Say, 1834)

Size: 12–25 mm.
Color: White, slightly iridescent.

Shape: Elongate, oblong; inequilateral.
Ornament or sculpture: Smooth except for microscopic growth lines; thin; posterior margin truncated and flexed to right, marked with radial ridge.
Hinge area: Umbones small, sharp; ligament small, brown; 2 cardinal teeth in left valve and 1 in right; 1 posterior lateral tooth.
Pallial line & interior: Anterior adductor scar elongate, posterior rounded; pallial sinus nearly half confluent, almost reaching anterior scar.
Habitat: Open-bay margins; shallow hypersaline lagoons; infaunal.
Localities: Southeast.
Occurrence: Common.
Range: Bermuda; Cape Cod to Florida; Texas; Campeche Bank; West Indies; Brazil.
Remarks: Lives in muddy bottoms.

Subgenus *Psammacoma* Dall, 1900

Short Macoma
Macoma (Psammacoma) brevifrons
(Say, 1834)

Size: 25 mm.
Color: White to pale peach.
Shape: Oval; inequilateral.
Ornament or sculpture: Shell smooth except for fine growth lines; very weak radial ridge posteriorly.
Hinge area: Umbones small, pointed, anterior to middle; ligament brown, small, external; 2 cardinal teeth in each valve; posterior tooth in left much smaller than others; no lateral teeth.

Pallial line & interior: Scars and pallial line hardly visible; elongate anterior scar and small round posterior scar; pallial sinus large, rounded, almost confluent with pallial line.
Habitat: Near shore, possibly in bays; infaunal.
Localities: Entire.
Occurrence: Uncommon.
Range: North Carolina to Texas; Yucatán; Brazil.
Remarks: Much the same color and size as *Tellina tampaensis*, but shape and hinge area differ; until monograph on macomas is published, *M. brevifrons* and *M. aurora* will be considered synonymous on the basis of published descriptions.

Subgenus *Austromacoma* Leach, 1961

Constricted Macoma
Macoma (Austromacoma) constricta
(Bruguière, 1792)

Size: 25–63 mm.
Color: White.
Shape: Subquadrate; inequivalve; inequilateral.
Ornament or sculpture: Sculptured with irregular, fine, concentric growth lines; low radial ridge marks posterior slope, which is flexed to right.
Hinge area: Umbones rounded; ligament long, narrow; cardinal teeth weak; no laterals.
Pallial line & interior: Muscle scars and pallial line weak; 2 rather high muscle scars; pallial sinus extended to near anterior scar,

convex above and correspondingly curved below.
Habitat: Open-bay margins and centers; infaunal.
Localities: Entire.
Occurrence: Fairly common.
Range: Florida to Texas; Yucatán; West Indies; Surinam; Brazil.
Remarks: More tolerant of extremes in salinities and temperatures than other macomas on Florida coast; hole in figured specimen drilled by predatory gastropod.

Coquina Shell
Donax variabilis Say, 1822

Size: 12.7–19 mm.
Color: Variable; interior bright; white, yellow, pink, bluish, purple, mauve; often with rays of darker tones.
Shape: Unequally trigonal or wedge-shaped with prolonged posterior end.
Ornament or sculpture: Glossy with fine concentric growth lines and radial striae that become stronger towards posterior end. Inner margins crenulate.
Hinge area: Two cardinal and an anterior and a posterior tooth in each valve.
Pallial line & interior: Deep pallial sinus.
Habitat: Surf zone.
Localities: Entire.
Occurrence: Common.
Range: New York to south Florida and Texas.

Remarks: In spite of being small, they make a delicious chowder.

Family PSAMMOBIIDAE Fleming, 1828
Subfamily SANGUINOLARIINAE Grant & Gale, 1931

Genus *Sanguinolaria* Lamarck, 1799

Atlantic Sanguin
Sanguinolaria sanguinolenta
(Gmelin, 1791)

Size: 38–50 mm.
Color: White; umbones and area just below bright orangish red fading into white ventrally.
Shape: Subovate; inequivalve; inequilateral.
Ornament or sculpture: Thin, gaping shell sculptured with microscopic growth lines; left valve slightly more compressed than right.
Hinge area: Hinge teeth near center of dorsal margin; 2 small cardinals in each valve; ligament external.
Pallial line & interior: Large pallial sinus with U-shaped hump at top.
Habitat: Offshore; infaunal.
Localities: South.
Occurrence: Uncommon.
Range: Southern Florida; Gulf states; West Indies; Surinam; almost all of Brazil.
Remarks: Color fades quickly; probably adventitious; wrongly referred to as *S. cruenta* (Lightfoot, 1786).

Subfamily PSAMMOBINAE Fleming, 1828

Genus *Asaphis* Fleming, 1828

Gaudy Asaphis
Asaphis deflorata (Linné, 1758)

Family SEMELIDAE Stoliczka, 1870

Genus *Semele* Schumacher, 1817

Cancellate Semele
Semele bellastriata (Conrad, 1837)

Size: 5 cm.
Color: Variable; yellow, whitish, stained with rose, red or purple; brighter inside.
Shape: Oblong, gaping posteriorly, moderately inflated.
Ornament or sculpture: Numerous, coarse, radiating threads.
Hinge area: Two prominent cardinal teeth in each valve; beaks inflated and rolled under themselves.
Pallial line & interior: Pallial sinus large, rounded in front.
Habitat: Intertidal sand.
Localities: South.
Occurrence: Uncommon.
Range: South Florida and West Indies; Bermuda; Brazilian oceanic islands.
Remarks: Syn. *Venus deflorata* (Linné, 1758)

Size: 12–18 mm.
Color: Yellowish white with reddish flecks or all purplish gray; interior white suffused with mauve or purple.
Shape: Oval.
Ornament or sculpture: Surface sculptured with concentric ridges and radial riblets stronger on anterior and posterior slopes, giving cancellate appearance at these extremities.
Hinge area: Umbones slightly pointed, just behind center; horizontal chondrophore and 2 cardinal teeth in each valve; right valve has 2 lateral teeth.
Pallial line & interior: 2 rounded muscle scars; pallial sinus deep, rounded.
Habitat: Offshore; infaunal.
Localities: Probably west, south, and Keys.
Occurrence: Uncommon beach shell.
Range: Bermuda; North Carolina to southern half of Florida; Texas; Campeche Bank; Yucatán; West Indies; Surinam; northeastern Brazil.
Remarks: Found after severe cold fronts.

White Atlantic Semele
Semele proficua (Pulteney, 1799)

Purplish Semele
Semele purpurascens (Gmelin, 1791)

Size: 12–35 mm.
Color: Whitish to yellowish white; interior yellowish, glossy, sometimes flecked with mauve.
Shape: Orbicular; equivalve.
Ornament or sculpture: Sculpture of fine, irregular growth lines and microscopic radial lines.
Hinge area: Umbones almost central, pointed; hinge area has long chondrophore to house resilium, 2 small, fragile cardinal teeth; right valve has 2 lateral teeth.
Pallial line & interior: Muscle scars rounded; pallial sinus deep, rounded, oblique.
Habitat: Open-bay centers, inlet areas, near shore; infaunal.
Localities: Entire.
Occurrence: Fairly common.
Range: Bermuda; North Carolina to southern half of Florida; Texas; Yucatán; Central America; West Indies; Brazilian coast to Argentina.
Remarks: The Panamic vicariant is *S. lenticularis* Sowerby, 1833.

Size: 25–38 mm.
Color: Variable: cream with purplish or orange flecks.
Shape: Oval; equivalve.
Ornament or sculpture: Thin shell sculptured with concentric striae weaker toward posterior margin; microscopic lines between striae but no radial ribs; lines tend to converge.
Hinge area: Umbones posterior of center, pointed; hinge with horizontal chondrophore, 2 cardinal teeth; right valve has 2 lateral teeth.
Pallial line & interior: Muscle scars irregularly shaped; pallial sinus deep, rounded.
Habitat: Offshore on sand bottoms and banks; infaunal.
Localities: South and west.
Occurrence: Fairly common.
Range: North Carolina to southern half of Florida; Texas; southern Mexico; Central America; West Indies; Brazilian coast to Uruguay.
Remarks: Very colorful.

Genus *Abra* Lamarck, 1818
Subgenus *Abra* s.s.

Common Atlantic Abra
Abra (Abra) aequalis (Say, 1822)

Genus *Cumingia* G. B. Sowerby I, 1833

Tellin-Like Cumingia
Cumingia tellinoides (Conrad, 1831)

Size: 6 mm.
Color: White.
Shape: Orbicular.
Ornament or sculpture: Smooth, polished; anterior margin of right valve grooved.
Hinge area: Umbones small, pointed; 2 small cardinal teeth in right valve, 1 weak; lateral teeth absent in left valve, 1 anterior lateral in right valve; elongate chondrophore extending posteriorly from cardinal teeth.
Pallial line & interior: Pallial sinus large, directed forward and upward.
Habitat: Open bays, inlet-influenced areas, along shore; infaunal.
Localities: Entire.
Occurrence: Common.
Range: Delaware to Florida; Texas; Gulf of Campeche; Yucatán; West Indies; Surinam; northeastern and eastern Brazil.
Remarks: Following severe cold fronts vast numbers are washed ashore.

Size: 12–18 mm.
Color: White.
Shape: Trigonal.
Ornament or sculpture: Thin shell sculptured with fine, slightly raised growth lines; posterior end slightly pointed, flexed; radial ridge on posterior slope.
Hinge area: Umbones pointed, just posterior to center; both valves have 1 small, bladelike cardinal tooth, 1 central spoon-shaped chondrophore, elongated anterior and posterior laterals.
Pallial line & interior: Anterior adductor scar elongated, posterior scar rounded; latter largely confluent with pallial line below; pallial sinus deep, rounded.
Habitat: Bay margins, high-salinity bays, inlet areas; infaunal.
Localities: North.
Occurrence: Fairly common.
Range: Nova Scotia to St. Augustine, Florida; Texas; Cuba.
Remarks: Dead specimens found in holes in rock and oyster shell but more apt to be found in mud among roots.

Family SOLECURTIDAE Orbigny, 1846
Subfamily SOLECURTINAE Orbigny, 1846

Genus *Solecurtus* Blainville, 1824

Corrugated Razor Clam
Solecurtus cumingianus Dunker, 1861

Genus *Tagelus* Gray, 1847
Subgenus *Mesopleura* Conrad, 1867

Purplish Tagelus
Tagelus (Mesopleura) divisus
(Spengler, 1794)

Size: 25–63 mm.
Color: White, dull.
Shape: Elongate cylindrical, flattened; equivalve.
Ornament or sculpture: Surface of shell sculptured with irregular growth lines crossed by fine, oblique lines; both rounded ends gape.
Hinge area: External ligament posterior to umbones; right valve has 2 strong cardinal teeth, left valve 1 cardinal tooth.
Pallial line & interior: Pallial sinus extends forward to point below cardinal teeth.
Habitat: Offshore; infaunal.
Localities: Northwest.
Occurrence: Uncommon beach shell.
Range: Southeastern United States; Texas; Mexico; Campeche Bank; West Indies; Colombia; Brazil.
Remarks: Usually only single valves on beach.

Size: 25–38 mm.
Color: Whitish purple with strong purple radial streak about midshell.
Shape: Flattened cylindrical, elongate; equivalve.
Ornament or sculpture: Thin, fragile shell unsculptured, gaping at both ends.
Hinge area: Umbones posterior of center, suppressed; cardinal but no lateral teeth in each valve; purple ray marks position of weak, internal radial rib just anterior to teeth.
Pallial line & interior: 2 muscle scars; pallial sinus deep but does not extend to cardinal teeth.
Habitat: Open sounds, open-lagoon margins; infaunal.
Localities: Entire.
Occurrence: Common.
Range: Bermuda; Cape Cod to southern Florida; Gulf states; Yucatán; Quintana Roo; Caribbean to Brazil; Surinam.
Remarks: A favored food of herons.

Stout Tagelus
Tagelus (Mesopleura) plebeius
(Lightfoot, 1786)

Size: 50–68 mm.
Color: White.
Shape: Elongate, rectangular; equivalve.
Ornament or sculpture: Strong shell sculptured with faint, irregular growth lines; gapes at each end; weak radial ridge on posterior slope.
Hinge area: Umbones posterior of center, suppressed; cardinal but no lateral teeth in each valve; lacks internal ribs of *T. divisus.*
Pallial line & interior: 2 muscle scars; pallial sinus deep.
Habitat: Enclosed lagoons, bay margins; infaunal.
Localities: Entire.
Occurrence: Common.
Range: Cape Cod to southern Florida; Gulf states; West Indies; Surinam; Brazilian coast to Bahia Blanca, Argentina.
Remarks: Buried in mud among roots; tolerates lower salinities than *T. divisus;* syn. *T. gibbus* Spengler, 1794.

Superfamily DREISSENACEA Gray, 1840
Family DREISSENIDAE Gray, 1840

Genus *Mytilopsis* Conrad, 1858

Conrad's False Mussel
Mytilopsis leucophaeta (Conrad, 1831)

Size: 18 mm.
Color: Bluish brown to tan.
Shape: Mussellike.
Ornament or sculpture: Exterior very rough; anterior end much depressed; byssal opening small; shelf, or septum, at beak end.
Hinge area: Long thin bar under ligament.
Pallial line & interior: Pallial line simple with 2 adductor muscle scars.
Habitat: Brackish water; epifaunal.
Localities: Entire.
Occurrence: Fairly common.
Range: New York to Florida to Texas and Mexico.
Remarks: Internal septum across end distinguishes it from mussel; attaches in clusters by byssal thread; [*Congeria leucophaeta*].

Superfamily CORBICULACEA Gray, 1847
Family CORBICULIDAE Gray, 1847

Genus *Polymesoda* Rafinesque, 1820

Carolina Marsh Clam
Polymesoda caroliniana (Bosc, 1802)

Subgenus *Pseudocyrena* Bourguignat, 1854

Florida Marsh Clam
Polymesoda (Pseudocyrena) maritima
   (Orbigny, 1842)

Size: 25–38 mm.
Color: White.
Shape: Trigonal, inflated; equivalve;
inequilateral.
Ornament or sculpture: Rather smooth
with weak concentric growth lines.
Hinge area: Erosion of umbones typical;
umbones elevated; each hinge with 3 small,
almost vertical, equally sized teeth below
umbones and each hinge with 1 anterior
and posterior lateral; dark brown, long,
narrow ligament external.
Pallial line & interior: Pallial sinus narrow,
ascending, fairly deep with 2 equal
adductor muscle scars.
Habitat: Estuaries; infaunal.
Localities: Northwest.
Occurrence: Fairly common.
Range: Virginia to northern half of Florida
and Texas.
Remarks: Can stand very brackish to fresh
water; common at mouths of tidal rivers.

Size: 25 mm.
Color: Whitish flushed with purple pink;
interior white with wide purple margin or
all purple.
Shape: Trigonal; equivalve; inequilateral.
Ornament or sculpture: Smooth with
weak, irregular growth lines; not heavy;
ventral margin slightly sinuate posteriorly.
Hinge area: Each hinge with 3 small almost
vertical teeth below umbones and each
hinge with 1 anterior and posterior lateral.
Pallial line & interior: Pallial sinus narrow,
ascending, fairly deep with 2 adductor
muscle scars.
Habitat: In sand in open hypersaline bays
and inlets; infaunal.
Localities: Northwest.
Occurrence: Common.
Range: Key West to northern Florida;
Texas; Yucatán; Quintana Roo.
Remarks: Syn. *Pseudocyrena floridana*
(Conrad, 1846).

Superfamily VENERACEA
Rafinesque, 1815
Family VENERIDAE Rafinesque, 1815
Subfamily PITARINAE Stewart, 1930

Genus *Callocardia* A. Adams, 1864
Subgenus *Agriopoma* Dall, 1902

Texas Venus
Callocardia (Agriopoma) texasiana
(Dall, 1892)

Size: 38–76 mm.
Color: Creamy white to dirty gray; interior chalky white.
Shape: Oval elongate, inflated; equivalve; inequilateral.
Ornament or sculpture: Smooth with only very fine concentric growth lines.
Hinge area: Umbones prominent, rolled in under themselves; weak, tear-shaped lunule; 3 cardinal teeth; posterior cardinal S-shaped in right valve; left anterior lateral small and fitting into socket in right valve.
Pallial line & interior: 2 small muscle scars, anterior scar very close to margin; pallial line strong with deep, triangular sinus touching posterior scar; margin smooth.
Habitat: Clay lagoon centers and along shore in clay; infaunal.
Localities: Northwest.
Occurrence: Uncommon to rare.
Range: Northwestern Florida to Texas and Mexico.

Remarks: May be assigned to genus *Pitar;* lives just below sand; live specimens rare; holotype collected by Wuerdemann ca. 1856 from Galveston, Texas.

Genus *Callista* Poli, 1791
Subgenus *Macrocallista* Meek, 1876

Calico Clam
Callista (Macrocallista) maculata
(Linné, 1758)

Size: 3.8–6.3 cm.
Color: Cream with irregular, almost checkered, brown marks. Interior white.
Shape: Oval. Equivalve. Inequilateral.
Ornament or sculpture: Highly polished.
Hinge area: Umbones small. Lunule small, impressed. Two unequal cardinals. Short, blunt anterior lateral. Thin posterior lateral.
Pallial line & interior: Two muscle scars, posterior larger. Pallial sinus wider at base, angled at end. Margins smooth.
Habitat: Offshore. Infaunal.
Localities: Entire?
Occurrence: Common.
Range: Southeastern United States; south Texas; Bermuda; Yucatán; West Indies; Brazil.

Remarks: This little beauty was originally *Venus maculata*.

Sunray Venus
Callista (Macrocallista) nimbosa
(Lightfoot, 1786)

Size: 101–127 mm.
Color: Pale salmon with broken, brownish radial lines.
Shape: Elongated oval; equivalve; inequilateral.
Ornament or sculpture: Polished; sculpture of inconspicuous radial and concentric lines.
Hinge area: Umbones depressed; lunule impressed, oval, purplish; long external ligament; 3 cardinal teeth.
Pallial line & interior: 2 muscle scars; pallial sinus reflected, wider at base, angled at end; margins smooth.
Habitat: Shallow sandy bottoms, inlet-influenced areas; infaunal.
Localities: Northwest.
Occurrence: Fairly common.
Range: North Carolina to Florida and Gulf states.
Remarks: Live buried in the sand; storms often wash them up.

Subfamily DOSINIINAE Deshayes, 1853

Genus *Dosinia* Scopoli, 1777

Disk Dosinia
Dosinia discus (Reeve, 1850)

Size: 50–76 mm.
Color: White.
Shape: Lenticular, flattened; equivalve; inequilateral.
Ornament or sculpture: Sculpture of numerous fine, concentric ridges.
Hinge area: Lunule heart-shaped; ligament strong, placed in groove; 3 cardinal teeth in each valve.
Pallial line & interior: Interior smooth, glossy; 2 small muscle scars connected by pallial line with large, angular sinus extending to center of shell.
Habitat: Near shore from 3.6 to 21.6 meters (2 to 12 fathoms); infaunal.
Localities: Northwest.
Occurrence: Common.
Range: Virginia to Florida; Gulf states; Mexico; Bahamas.
Remarks: Pairs held together by strong ligament; commonly wash ashore in winter; often neat holes drilled by predatory gastropod present.

Elegant Dosinia
Dosinia elegans Conrad, 1846

Subfamily CYCLININAE Frizzell, 1936

Genus *Cyclinella* Dall, 1902

Atlantic Cyclinella
Cyclinella tenuis (Récluz, 1852)

Size: 50–76 mm.
Color: Ivory.
Shape: Lenticular, flattened; equivalve; inequilateral.
Ornament or sculpture: Sculpture of regular concentric ribs, fewer in number and heavier than in *D. discus.*
Hinge area: Umbones prominent; lunule small, partly submarginal; 3 cardinal teeth in each valve with lateral teeth present; left middle cardinal and right posterior cardinal bifid.
Pallial line & interior: 2 muscle scars connected by pallial line with long, angular sinus touching posterior scar; margins smooth.
Habitat: Offshore; infaunal.
Localities: Entire.
Occurrence: Fairly common.
Range: South Carolina; Florida; south Texas to Isla Mujeres; Yucatán.
Remarks: May be syn. of *D. concentrica* (Born, 1778).

Size: 25–50 mm.
Color: Whitish.
Shape: Circular, flattened; equivalve; inequilateral.
Ornament or sculpture: Resembles *Dosinia* but smaller and more thin shelled; surface sculptured with very fine, irregular growth lines.
Hinge area: Submarginal hinge ligament; 3 cardinal teeth but no laterals as *Dosinia* have; right posterior tooth bifid.
Pallial line & interior: 2 muscle scars; anterior scar much nearer ventral margin than that of *Dosinia*; pallial sinus ascending, long, narrow; margins smooth.
Habitat: Inlet-influenced areas and bay margins; infaunal.
Localities: Entire?
Occurrence: Fairly common.
Range: Eastern United States; Texas; West Indies; Surinam; Brazil.
Remarks: Easily mistaken for *Dosinia* but much smaller.

Subfamily GEMMINAE Dall, 1902

Genus *Gemma* Deshayes, 1853

Amethyst Gem Clam
Gemma cf. *G. purpurea* Lea, 1842

Remarks: One of smallest bivalves; easily overlooked; tentative identity of figured specimen not checked by expert; may be *Gemma gemma* (Totten, 1834).

Subfamily CHIONINAE Frizzell, 1936

Genus *Chione* Megerle von Mühlfeld, 1811

Cross-Barred Venus
Chione cancellata (Linné, 1767)

Size: 3 mm.
Color: Whitish with purple on umbones and posterior areas.
Shape: Rounded trigonal.
Ornament or sculpture: Glossy with numerous, fine, concentric ribs.
Hinge area: Lunule large; 2 large teeth in left valve with socket between, 3 teeth in right valve.
Pallial line & interior: Small muscle scars; pallial sinus points upward, triangular; inner margin faintly crenulate.
Habitat: In shallow water, sandy bottom; infaunal.
Localities: Not determined.
Occurrence: Common?
Range: Nova Scotia to Florida; Texas; Yucatán; Bahamas; introduced to Puget Sound.

Size: 25–27 mm.
Color: White to gray, often rayed with brown; interior glossy white with blue purple.
Shape: Ovate to subtrigonal; equivalve; inequilateral.
Ornament or sculpture: Surface sculptured with numerous strong, bladelike concentric ridges and many radial ribs; when concentric ridges beachworn, pattern appears very cancellate; heavy, porcelaneous.
Hinge area: Escutcheon long, smooth, V-shaped; lunule heart-shaped; 3 cardinal teeth in each valve; no anterior laterals.
Pallial line & interior: 2 muscle scars connected by pallial line with very small, triangular pallial sinus; margins crenulate.
Habitat: Open bays, bay margins, inlet-influenced areas; infaunal.
Localities: Entire.
Occurrence: Common.
Range: North Carolina to Florida; Texas; Gulf of Mexico to Quintana Roo; Costa

Rica; West Indies; Brazil; Brazilian oceanic islands.
Remarks: *c. mazyckii* Dall, 1902 is another form.

Lady-in-Waiting Venus
Chione intapurpurea (Conrad, 1849)

Size: 25–38 mm.
Color: Glossy white to cream, often with irregular brown marks; interior white or with purple splotch in posterior third.
Shape: Ovate to subtrigonal, inflated; equivalve; inequilateral.
Ornament or sculpture: Sculpture of numerous low, rounded concentric ribs; ribs marked with tiny serrations at lower edge that give interspaces beaded appearance; rib on posterior slope lamellate.
Hinge area: Lunule heart-shaped with raised lamellations; escutcheon with fine transverse lines; ligament exterior; 3 cardinal teeth in each valve, no laterals.
Pallial line & interior: 2 shiny muscle scars connected by pallial line with short, narrow, oblique sinus.
Habitat: Near shore, 3.6 to 21.6 meters (2 to 12 fathoms); infaunal.
Localities: Entire.
Occurrence: Fairly common beach shell.
Range: Chesapeake Bay to Florida; Texas; Yucatán; West Indies; Brazil.

Remarks: A purplish starfish has been reported feeding on these in southwestern Florida.

Imperial Venus
Chione latilirata (Conrad, 1841)

Size: 2.5 cm.
Color: Cream with rose and brown markings.
Shape: Trigonal-ovate, solid.
Ornament or sculpture: 5–9 glossy, concentric folds across disk.
Hinge area: Heart shaped lunule.
Pallial line & interior: Two muscle scars connected by pallial sinus.
Habitat: Shallow water in sand.
Localities: Entire.
Occurrence: Uncommon.
Range: North Carolina to Florida; to Texas; Brazil.
Remarks: Burrow just beneath the surface.

Subgenus *Timoclea* Brown, 1827
Gray Pygmy Venus
Chione (Timoclea) grus (Holmes, 1858)

Genus *Mercenaria* Schumacher, 1817
Southern Quahog
Mercenaria campechiensis (Gmelin, 1791)

Size: 6–9 mm.
Color: Grayish white, often with pink cast; interior with broad ray of purple at posterior end.
Shape: Oblong; inequivalve; inequilateral.
Ornament or sculpture: 30 to 40 fine, radial ribs crossed by finer, concentric threads; more heavily sculptured on posterior and anterior margins.
Hinge area: Lunule narrow, heart shaped, colored brown; escutcheon narrow, sunken; 3 cardinal teeth in each valve.
Pallial line & interior: 2 muscle scars connected by weak pallial line with small, oblique sinus; margins crenulate.
Habitat: Offshore in intermediate shelf assemblage; sand and shell bottom; infaunal.
Localities: Entire.
Occurrence: Common.
Range: North Carolina to Key West to Louisiana; Texas to Cabo Catoche, Mexico; Quintana Roo.
Remarks: This tiny Venus is hard to find.

Size: 76–152 mm.
Color: Dirty gray to whitish; interior white, rarely with purple blotches; porcelaneous.
Shape: Ovate trigonal, inflated; equivalve; inequilateral.
Ornament or sculpture: Sculpture of numerous concentric growth lines, farther apart near beaks; shell very heavy.
Hinge area: Lunule as wide as long; 3 cardinals in each valve; left middle cardinal split.
Pallial line & interior: 2 muscle scars connected by pallial line with small, angular sinus.
Habitat: Offshore; infaunal.
Localities: Entire.
Occurrence: Common.
Range: Chesapeake Bay to Florida; Texas; Yucatán; Cuba.
Remarks: Not been used commercially as has its northern relative, *M. mercenaria*.

Genus *Anomalocardia* Schumacher, 1817

Pointed Venus
Anomalocardia auberiana (Orbigny, 1842)

Family PETRICOLIDAE Deshayes, 1831

Genus *Petricola* Lamarck, 1801
Subgenus *Petricolaria* Stoliczka, 1870

False Angel Wing
Petricola (Petricolaria) pholadiformis
(Lamarck, 1818)

Size: 12–18 mm.
Color: Variable: from white to tan with brown rays; interior white with purplish brown at posterior margin.
Shape: Wedge-shaped; equivalve; inequilateral.
Ornament or sculpture: Glossy surface sculptured with rounded concentric ridges and very faint radial lines; posterior slope slightly rostrate.
Hinge area: Umbones small; lunule distinct; escutcheon depressed; 3 cardinal teeth in each valve; right anterior cardinal small and in horizontal position.
Pallial line & interior: 2 muscle scars connected by pallial line and small, angular sinus; margins crenulate.
Habitat: Both enclosed and open hypersaline lagoons; infaunal.
Localities: South.
Occurrence: Common.
Range: Southern half of Florida; Texas; Yucatán; Quintana Roo; Central America; West Indies; Brazil to Uruguay.
Remarks: Can withstand high salinity; syn. *A. cuneimeris* Conrad, 1846.

Size: Up to 50 mm.
Color: White.
Shape: Elongate, somewhat cylindrical.
Ornament or sculpture: Sculpture of numerous radial ribs and fine growth lines, diminishing posteriorly on fragile shell; anterior ribs prominently scaled.
Hinge area: Umbones low, near anterior end; small, brown ligament just posterior to umbones; 3 cardinal teeth long, pointed in left valve, 2 in right.
Pallial line & interior: Both adductor muscle scars somewhat rounded; pallial sinus fairly narrow and deep with rounded end.
Habitat: Open-bay margins, inlet-influenced areas, near shore in clay banks; infaunal.
Localities: Entire.
Occurrence: Common.
Range: Gulf of St. Lawrence to Gulf of Mexico; Brazil to Uruguay.
Remarks: Easily confused with *Pholas*; check teeth.

Subgenus *Pseudoirus* Habe, 1951

Atlantic Rupellaria
Petricola (Pseudoirus) typica (Jonas, 1844)

Order MYOIDEA Stoliczka, 1870
Suborder MYINA Newell, 1965
Superfamily MYACEA Lamarck, 1809
Family MYIDAE Lamarck, 1809

Genus *Paramya* Conrad, 1861

Paramya subovata (Conrad, 1845)

Size: 25 mm.
Color: White.
Shape: Oblong, variable; inequilateral.
Ornament or sculpture: Rather heavy shell sculptured with irregularly spaced radial ribs, narrower over anterior area; valves gape posteriorly.
Hinge area: Umbones rounded, not prominent, curved forward; 3 cardinal teeth in left valve, 2 in right.
Pallial line & interior: Pallial sinus semicircular, somewhat longer than posterior adductor scar.
Habitat: Jetties and offshore; infaunal.
Localities: Entire?
Occurrence: Fairly common.
Range: North Carolina to southern half of Florida; Texas; Yucatán; West Indies; Brazil.
Remarks: Shape of this coral- and rock-dwelling bivalve variable, conforming to dwelling place; [*Rupellaria typica*].

Size: 5–10 mm.
Color: Grayish white.
Shape: Subquadrate.
Ornament or sculpture: Concentric growth lines and microscopic granules near edge of valves.
Hinge area: Chondrophore in either valve.
Pallial line & interior: Polished; pallial line simple, hardly discernible; large, highly polished, pear-shaped muscle scar near dorsal area.
Habitat: Offshore; commensal with echiuroid worm, *Thalassema hartmani.*
Localities: Northwest.
Occurrence: Uncommon.
Range: Delaware to Florida; Texas.
Remarks: Found with echeuroidamus (*Thalassema hartmani*).

Family CORBULIDAE Lamarck, 1818
Subfamily CORBULINAE Gray, 1823

Genus *Corbula* Bruguière, 1797

Caribbean Corbula
Corbula cf. *C. caribaea* d'Orbigny, 1842

(completed second growth stage)

(first growth stage)

(mature)

Size: 9 mm.
Color: White.
Shape: Subovoid, very solid; inequivalve;
slightly inequilateral; posterior acutely
rostrate; anterior well rounded and
globose; dorsal margins nearly straight and
ventral margin excurved.

(beginning second growth stage)

Ornament or sculpture: Irregular concentric ridges and striae; larger valve sculptured more regularly and deeply than other, with minute radiating striae in young.

Hinge area: Beaks small, not involute; umbones very convex, indistinctly angulated anteriorly, with sharp but not very prominent angle posteriorly; stout teeth.

Pallial line & interior: Simple; 2 small muscle scars.

Habitat: Muddy bottom in bays and offshore.

Localities: Entire?

Occurrence: Common?

Range: North Carolina; Florida; West Indies; Surinam to Brazil.

Remarks: Literature abounds with confusion concerning the genus *Corbula*; to add my bit: figured specimens may or may not be *C. caribaea*, syn. *C. swiftiana* C. B. Adams, 1852, and may be *C. barrattiana* C. B. Adams, 1852; group of figures helps explain dilemma.

Size: 9 mm.

Color: Whitish.

Shape: Subtrigonal, inflated; inequivalve.

Ornament or sculpture: Sculpture of strong, concentric ridges; right valve larger than left, more inflated, stronger sculpture.

Hinge area: Umbones high, almost central, curved in; right valve has single prominent cardinal tooth; left valve has corresponding socket; ligament internal.

Pallial line & interior: 2 small roundish muscle scars; pallial line well impressed; pallial sinus but slight sinuation in pallial line.

Habitat: Offshore, 36 to 62 meters (20 to 40 fathoms); infaunal.

Localities: Entire?

Occurrence: Uncommon?

Range: North Carolina to Gulf of Mexico; West Indies; northern and northeastern Brazil.

Remarks: Common outer-beach *Corbula*, sometimes found in bamboo-root clumps; commensal with Foraminifera; *C. krebsiana* C. B. Adams, 1852, may be same.

Subgenus *Varicorbula* Grant & Gale, 1931

Oval Corbula
Corbula (Varicorbula) operculata (Philippi, 1849)

Superfamily GASTROCHAENACEA Gray, 1840
Family GASTROCHAENIDAE Gray, 1840

Genus *Gastrochaena* Spengler, 1783

Atlantic Rocellaria
Gastrochaena hians (Gmelin, 1791)

Size: 12–18 mm.
Color: White.

Shape: Petal-shaped.

Ornament or sculpture: Sculpture of low, indistinct, fine, concentric lines; posterior end large, rounded; entire ventral-anterior end gaping to accommodate foot.

Hinge area: Umbones low; hinge area weak with 1 large toothlike structure in umbonal cavity.

Pallial line & interior: Posterior adductor scar large; anterior scar degenerate; pallial sinus deep, angular.

Habitat: Offshore; infaunal.

Localities: Entire.

Occurrence: Uncommon in beach drift.

Range: Bermuda; North Carolina to Florida; Texas; Yucatán; West Indies; Surinam; northeastern and eastern Brazil.

Remarks: Constructs hollow "cell" of sand and bits of shell glued together in which it lives; often found inside empty pecten shells; [*Rocellaria hians*].

Superfamily HIATELLACEA Gray, 1824
Family HIATELLIDAE Gray, 1824

Genus *Hiatella* Daudin, 1801

Arctic Saxicave
Hiatella arctica (Linné, 1767)

Size: 25 mm.

Color: Chalky white.

Shape: Irregularly oblong.

Ornament or sculpture: Sculpture of coarse, irregular growth lines; weak radial rib on posterior end, may be scaled; posterior may gape.

Hinge area: Umbones close together and about one-third back from anterior end; teeth indefinite.

Pallial line & interior: Pallial line discontinuous; sinus large but irregular.

Habitat: Inlet areas, hypersaline lagoons, offshore; boring infaunal.

Localities: Entire.

Occurrence: Fairly common.

Range: Arctic seas to deep waters in West Indies; Yucatán; Brazil; Pacific.

Remarks: Nestling and boring habits cause shape and sculpture to vary greatly.

Genus *Panopea* Menard de la Groye, 1807

Geoduck
Panopea bitruncata (Conrad, 1872)

Size: 127–228 mm.

Color: White.

Shape: Quadrate, elongated.

Ornament or sculpture: Sculpture of concentric, wavy growth lines; valves gape at both ends.

Hinge area: Umbones low, incurved, almost central; 1 large single, simple "tooth" and broad ledge to which ligament attached.

Pallial line & interior: Anterior adductor muscle scar elongated; posterior rounded, small; pallial sinus short, rounded.

Habitat: Offshore and inlet areas; boring infaunal.

Localities: Entire?

Occurrence: Rare beach shell.

Range: North Carolina to Florida and south Texas.

Remarks: Seldom found alive or dead because lives so deep in substratum that valves rarely wash out of burrows.

Suborder PHOLADINA Newell, 1965
Superfamily PHOLADACEA
    Lamarck, 1809
Family PHOLADIDAE Lamarck, 1809
Subfamily PHOLADINAE Lamarck, 1809

Genus *Pholas* Linné, 1758
Subgenus *Thovana* Gray, 1847

Campeche Angel Wing
Pholas (Thovana) campechiensis (Gmelin, 1791)

Size: Up to 128 mm.
Color: White.
Shape: Subelliptical.
Ornament or sculpture: Thin, fragile shell sculptured with laminate, concentric ridges and radial ribs; sculpture becomes weaker posteriorly; shells gape; shells rounded at both ends.
Hinge area: Umbones prominent, located near anterior fourth of shell, covered by double septate umbonal reflections; apophyses delicate, short, broad, projecting beneath umbo at sharp posterior angle; 3 accessory plates: nearly rectangular protoplax, transverse mesoplax, elongate metaplax.
Pallial line & interior: Adductor muscle scars and pallial line well marked; pallial sinus wide, extending anteriorly almost two-thirds of distance to umbo.

Habitat: Offshore in wood and clay; boring infaunal.
Localities: Northwest.
Occurrence: Fairly common.
Range: North Carolina to Gulf states; Mexico; Costa Rica; West Indies; Surinam; Brazil to Uruguay; Senegal to Liberia.
Remarks: Common in beach drift but seldom found alive; at times found in wood on outer beaches; distinguished by comblike umbonal reflection; figured specimen filled with cotton.

Genus *Barnea* Risso, 1826

Fallen Angel Wing
Barnea truncata (Say, 1822)

Size: 71 mm.
Color: White.
Shape: Elongate elliptical.
Ornament or sculpture: Rather thin shell sculptured with radial ribs and concentric ridges; concentric ridges have lamella anteriorly, becoming weaker toward posterior end; radial ribs lacking on posterior slope; imbrications formed where concentric ridges cross radial ribs; shell beaked anteriorly and truncate posteriorly.
Hinge area: Umbones prominent, near anterior third; apophysis narrow, long, bladelike, curved; protoplax lanceolate, with posterior nucleus and definite growth lines.
Pallial line & interior: Pallial line and muscle scars well marked; pallial sinus almost as wide as shell is high, extending about halfway to umbones.
Habitat: In clay bottoms of bays; boring infaunal.
Localities: Entire.
Occurrence: Locally common.

Range: Massachusetts Bay to southern Florida; Texas; Surinam; eastern Brazil; Senegal.

Remarks: Siphons capable of extending 10 to 12 times length of shell; animal cannot withdraw into shell and usually lives in deep burrows in clay but known to live in wood also.

Genus *Cyrtopleura* Tryon, 1862
Subgenus *Scobinopholas* Grant & Gale, 1931

Angel Wing
Cyrtopleura (Scobinopholas) costata (Linné, 1758)

Size: 177 mm.
Color: White.
Shape: Elongate oval.
Ornament or sculpture: Rather light shell sculptured with concentric ridges and strong radial ribs that extend entire length of shell; where ribs cross concentric line, imbrications formed, stronger on anterior and posterior slopes.
Hinge area: Umbones prominent, located near anterior fourth of shell; umbones well separated from raised umbonal reflections; protoplax triangular in outline, mostly chitinous; mesoplax calcareous; apophyses large, spoon-shaped, hollow at upper end.
Pallial line & interior: Anterior and posterior muscle scars fairly well marked, but pallial sinus not evident.
Habitat: Open-bay margins, inlet-influenced areas; boring infaunal.
Localities: South. Rare in northwest.
Occurrence: Common.

Range: Massachusetts to Florida; Texas; Mexico; West Indies; Surinam; Brazilian coast to Paraná.

Remarks: Bores into clay substratum in bays to depth of about 46 centimeters (18 inches); inability to withdraw into shell makes it very susceptible to changes of salinity; [*Pholas costata*].

Subfamily MARTESIINAE Grant & Gale, 1931

Genus *Martesia* G. B. Sowerby I, 1824
Subgenus *Martesia* s.s.

Fragile Martesia
Martesia (Martesia) fragilis Verrill & Bush, 1890

Size: 18 mm.
Color: White.
Shape: Pear-shaped.
Ornament or sculpture: Valves divided into 2 sections by shallow umbonal-ventral sulcus; anterior part sculptured with concentric, denticulated ridges and weak radial ribs; posterior part sculptured with smooth, rounded ridges; truncated beaks gape; shell rounded, closed posteriorly.
Hinge area: Umbones prominent, located near anterior end of shell in adults; mesoplax circular to oval, depressed with

strong concentric sculpture; metaplax long, narrow, pointed anteriorly, wider and rounded posteriorly; apophyses long, thin, extending under umbones anteriorly at angle.

Pallial line & interior: Muscle scars strong; pallial sinus wide, deep, extending almost to umbonal-ventral ridge.

Habitat: Pelagic in floating wood; boring infaunal.

Localities: Entire.

Occurrence: Common.

Range: Bermuda; Virginia south through Gulf of Mexico; West Indies to Brazil; Surinam; Pacific coast of Mexico; Indo-Pacific.

Remarks: Easily confused with *M. striata;* however, mesoplax depressed, has concentric sculpture, and has sharply keeled edges.

Subgenus *Particoma* Bartsch & Rehder, 1945

Wedge-Shaped Martesia
Martesia (Particoma) cuneiformis (Say, 1822)

Size: 12–21 mm.

Color: White.

Shape: Pear-shaped.

Ornament or sculpture: Valves divided into parts by narrow, umbonal-ventral sulcus; anterior part sculptured with concentric, denticulated ridges; posterior part sculptured with smooth, rounded, concentric ridges, weak growth lines; shell gapes anteriorly, rounded, closed posteriorly.

Hinge area: Umbones prominent, located near anterior end of shell; umbonal reflection small, adpressed, not free; mesoplax cuneiform, or wedge-shaped, with median groove and radiating growth lines; metaplax long, narrow, divided; apophyses long, thin, almost parallel with umbonal-ventral ridge.

Pallial line & interior: Muscle scars well marked; posterior adductor scar long, oval; anterior scar kidney-shaped; pallial sinus broad, extending anteriorly beyond umbonal-ventral ridge.

Habitat: Pelagic in wood; boring infaunal.

Localities: Entire.

Occurrence: Fairly common.

Range: Southeastern United States; Texas; West Indies; Brazil; Pacific Panama.

Remarks: Easily confused with *Diplothyra smithii* Tryon, 1862, unless characteristic wedge-shaped mesoplax present; material in which animal bores readily affects shape of genus, causing some problem in identification.

Genus *Diplothyra* Tryon, 1862

Oyster Piddock
Diplothyra smithii Tryon, 1862

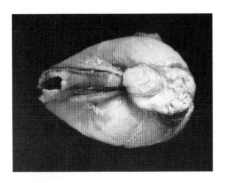

Quilling's Jouannetia
Jouannetia quillingi R. D. Turner, 1955

Size: 15 mm.
Color: White.
Shape: Pear-shaped.
Ornament or sculpture: Divided into 2 parts by umbonal-ventral sulcus; anterior part triangular in shape, sculptured by fine, close-set, wavy, concentric ridges and numerous weak radial ribs; posterior part has only growth lines; widely gaping anteriorly; rounded, closed posteriorly.
Hinge area: Umbones prominent, near anterior fourth of shell; umbones imbedded in callum that extends posteriorly on either side of mesoplax; apophyses long, thin, fragile; large chondrophore in left valve; mesoplax divided into concentrically sculptured posterior section and wrinkled anterior section; mesoplax and hypoplax forked posteriorly.
Pallial line & interior: Adductor scars large; pallial sinus broad, deep, extending anteriorly past umbonal-ventral ridge.
Habitat: High-salinity oyster reefs; boring infaunal.
Localities: Northwest.
Occurrence: Common.
Range: Massachusetts south to Daytona Beach and Sanibel Island, Florida; west to Texas and Surinam.
Remarks: Similar in appearance to *Martesia cuneiformis* but not found in wood, preferring shell and coquina rock; bores into oyster shell but not commercially damaging; [*Martesia smithii*].

Size: 21 mm.
Color: White to gray.
Shape: Globose, pear-shaped.
Ornament or sculpture: Valves divided into 2 parts by umbonal-ventral sulcus; anterior part triangular and sculptured with numerous laminate, imbricate, concentric ridges and weak radial ribs; shell constricted at sulcus; posterior part sculptured with thin, concentric ridges and growth lines; ridgs bear long, curved spines.
Hinge area: Umbones prominent, near anterior third of shell; umbonal reflections free, raised; callum extends dorsally between beaks, on left valve enlarged to form covering for anterior adductor muscle; mesoplax small, wedge-shaped; chondrophore on left valve.
Pallial line & interior: Muscle scars barely visible; pallial sinus extends anteriorly to umbonal-ventral ridge.
Habitat: In wood and calcareous rock offshore, pelagic; boring infaunal.
Localities: Entire?
Occurrence: Uncommon to rare.
Range: North Carolina to Lake Worth, Florida; Texas.
Remarks: Found in floating wood.

Family TEREDINIDAE Rafinesque, 1815
Subfamily TEREDININAE
Rafinesque, 1815

Genus Teredo Linné, 1758

Genus *Lyrodus* Binney, 1870

Stalked Shipworm
Lyrodus pedicellatus (Quatrefages, 1849)
[See *SST*, p. 258]

Subfamily BANKIINAE Turner, 1966

Genus *Bankia* Gray, 1842
Subgenus *Bankiella* Bartsch, 1921

Gould's Shipworm
Bankia (*Bankiella*) *gouldi* (Bartsch, 1908)

Bartsch's Shipworm
Teredo bartschi Clapp, 1923

(after R. D. Turner, *A survey and illustrated catalogue of the Teredinidae* [Cambridge, Mass.: Harvard Univ. Mus. Comp. Zool., 1966], p. 147)

Size: 27 mm.
Color: Pallets white.
Shape: Stalk long; blade short.
Ornament or sculpture: Blade deeply excavated at top.
Hinge area: None.
Pallial line & interior: None.
Habitat: Wood borer; infaunal.
Localities: Northwest.
Occurrence: Fairly common.
Range: Bermuda; South Carolina to northern half of Florida and Texas; introduced to Baja California.
Remarks: Pallets, not shell, used in identification.

(after Turner 1966, p. 247)

Size: 27 mm.
Color: White.
Shape: Pallet elongate.
Ornament or sculpture: Blade composed of numerous conelike elements on central stalk.
Hinge area: None.
Pallial line & interior: None.
Habitat: In wood, mangroves; boring infaunal.
Localities: Entire.
Occurrence: Common.
Range: New Jersey to Florida; Texas; Central America; West Indies; Brazil; Pacific coast of Mexico.
Remarks: Shells helpful in identification only when used in conjunction with pallets.

Subclass ANOMALODESMATA Dall, 1889
Order PHOLADOMYOIDEA
  Newell, 1965
Superfamily PANDORACEA
  Rafinesque, 1815
Family PANDORIDAE Rafinesque, 1815

Genus *Pandora* Bruguière, 1797
Subgenus *Clidophora* Carpenter, 1864

Say's Pandora
Pandora (Clidophora) trilineata Say, 1822

Size: 18–25 mm.
Color: White to cream; interior pearly.
Shape: Semilunar, flat; inequivalve;
inequilateral.
Ornament or sculpture: Flat, compressed
valves sculptured with microscopic,
concentric growth lines; left valve has radial
ridge along posterior slope; strong ridge
along hinge margin.
Hinge area: Umbones tiny, near rounded
anterior end; hinge internal just below
umbones; lamellar plates replace teeth.
Pallial line & interior: 2 small, round
adductor muscles; pallial line simple,
discontinuous.
Habitat: Inlet areas, open-sound and
lagoon centers in clayey sediments;
infaunal.
Localities: Entire.
Occurrence: Fairly common.
Range: Cape Hatteras to Florida; Texas.
Remarks: One wonders how any animal
finds space to live between the flat valves.

Family LYONSIIDAE Fischer, 1887

Genus *Lyonsia* Turton, 1822

Florida Lyonsia
Lyonsia floridana Conrad, 1848

Size: 16 mm.
Color: White, translucent.
Shape: Elongate, rather tear-shaped;
inequivalve; inequilateral.
Ornament or sculpture: Thin shell
sculptured with fine growth lines; valves
gape posteriorly.
Hinge area: Umbones tiny, pointed; no
teeth; small groove posterior to umbones
houses ligament.
Pallial line & interior: 2 adductor muscle
scars; pallial line indistinct.
Habitat: Open-bay margins, inlet areas, in
grass beds; infaunal.
Localities: West and northwest.
Occurrence: Fairly common.
Range: West coast of Florida; Texas;
Surinam.
Remarks: Byssal attachment.

Family PERIPLOMATIDAE Dall, 1895

Genus *Periploma* Schumacher, 1816

Unequal Spoon Clam
Periploma margaritaceum (Lamarck, 1801)

Size: 18–25 mm.
Color: White, translucent.
Shape: Subquadrate; inequivalve; inequilateral.
Ornament or sculpture: Sculpture of fine, concentric growth lines on rather fragile shell; posterior margin very truncate; low keel from umbones to anterior ventral margin.
Hinge area: Umbones small, near posterior end; ligament internal, located in spoon-shaped "tooth" in each valve.
Pallial line & interior: 2 small adductor muscle scars; pallial sinus broad, short, strongly defined.
Habitat: Open-sound, open-lagoon centers, inlet areas in sandy bottoms; infaunal.
Localities: Entire.
Occurrence: Common.
Range: South Carolina to Florida; Texas to Mexico; Costa Rica; West Indies; Brazil.
Remarks: Sporadically on outer beach in large numbers; valves often with holes bored by gastropod (reported to be *Marginella apicina*); syn. *P. inequale* (C. B. Adams, 1842)

Class SCAPHOPODA Bronn, 1862

Note: For help with DENTALIIDAE, try the various papers by Ruth Turner of Harvard University. Those photographed are what I found in Texas. I have none collected in Florida. They need further study.

Family DENTALIIDAE Gray, 1834

Genus *Dentalium* Linné, 1758
Subgenus *Paradentalium* Cotton &
Godfrey, 1933

Texas Tusk
Dentalium (Paradentalium) texasianum
Philippi, 1849

Ornament or sculpture: Hexagonal in cross section with 6 main ribs interspaced with numerous cordlike riblets on broad interspaces; apical pipe clearly visible unless tip broken off.
Aperture: Hexagonal.
Habitat: Open-bay margins, inlets, channel in stiff clay sediments; semi-infaunal.
Localities: Entire.
Occurrence: Common.
Range: North Carolina to Texas; Yucatán.
Remarks: Holotype collected by F. Roemer near Galveston, Texas, ca. 1846.

(apex)

Size: 18–35 mm.
Color: White.
Shape: Tapering cylinder; curved.

Subgenus *Antalis* H. & A. Adams, 1954
Dentalium cf. *(Antalis)* sp. A & B

(apex)

Size: Up to 28 mm.
Color: Whitish to pale amber.
Shape: Very slender, tapered cylinder; curved.
Ornament or sculpture: Microscopic longitudinal ribs at apical end of delicate shell; remainder of shell smooth except for growth rings; growth rings stronger than in *D.* cf. *(Laevidentalium)* sp. C; apical slit; some adult shells do not have microscopic lines.

Aperture: Round, simple.
Habitat: Inlet area [?]; semi-infaunal.
Localities: Central, south, probably entire.
Occurrence: Fairly common.
Range: Not defined.
Remarks: 2 specimens and details of apexes figured; may or may not be same species; I have examined some of same size, shape, and color which are completely smooth with apical slit, some with apical ribs and slit, and others with apical ribs and no slit; previously all *Dentaliums* in Texas without hexagonal cross section and heavy

ribs of *D. texasianum* reported as being one species, *D. eboreum* Conrad, 1846; Conrad described *D. eboreum* as having microscopic apical striae but *no* slit; if absence of slit in those I have examined is natural and not due to breakage, they could be *D. eboreum;* however, those with slit do not fit that description.

Subgenus *Laevidentalium* Cossmann, 1888

Dentalium cf. *(Laevidentalium)* sp. C

Ornament or sculpture: Smooth except for faint growth rings; no apical slit; cross section round.
Aperture: Round, simple.
Habitat: Inlet areas and near shore; semi-infaunal.
Localities: Central, south.
Occurrence: Fairly common.
Range: Not defined.
Remarks: Shell identified as *D. eboreum* in Andrews 1971 and referred to by other Texas malacologists as *D. eboreum* Conrad, 1846, but larger and has less definite growth rings; examination under microscope shows absence of longitudinal apical ribs typical of *D. eboreum.*

Family SIPHONODENTALIIDAE
   Simroth, 1894

Genus *Cadulus* Philippi, 1844
Subgenus *Gadila* Gray, 1847

Cadulus cf. *(Gadila)* sp. A

(apex)

Size: Up to 37 mm.
Color: White.
Shape: Tapered cylinder; curved.

Size: Up to 8 mm.
Color: White, smooth, glossy.
Shape: Cylinder; swollen in middle, tapering toward each end.
Ornament or sculpture: Smooth, polished.
Aperture: Round, simple.
Habitat: Near shore; semi-infaunal.
Localities: Entire.
Occurrence: Fairly common.
Range: Not determined.
Remarks: Shell mistakenly identified as *C. carolinensis* Bush, 1885, in Andrews 1971 and other literature on Texas shallow-water mollusks; typical "small, distinct notches, two on each side," described by Bush, absent in this small species, often abundant in beach drift; however, typical *C. carolinensis* found in deeper offshore waters; in addition to notches, has more oblique aperture than do specimens which wash up on beach.

Class CEPHALOPODA Cuvier, 1797

Subclass COLEOIDEA Bather, 1888
Order SEPIOIDEA Naef, 1916
Family SPIRULIDAE Owen, 1836

Genus *Spirula* Lamarck, 1799

Common Spirula
Spirula spirula (Linné, 1758)

Size: Animal 55 mm, shell 25 mm.
Color: Shell porcelaneous white; animal light brown.
Description: Closely coiled and chambered shell enclosed in posterior end of cylindrical body; 2 folds cover coiled shell, visible dorsally and ventrally but completely enclosed within mantle; posterior end of body truncate with 2 lateral fins; circular disc between fins emits light; 2 eyes in large head protrude beyond mantle edges; arms short, stout, pointed, with 4 rows of suckers; tentacles short with numerous rows of minute suckers.
Habitat: Offshore in deep waters.
Localities: Entire.
Occurrence: Common.
Range: Worldwide.
Remarks: Coiled shell often on outer beaches by thousands; normal position for animal is vertical with arms hanging down; living mollusk seldom seen.

Order TEUTHOIDEA Naef, 1916
Suborder MYOPSIDA Orbigny, 1840
Family LOLIGINIDAE Orbigny, 1841

Genus *Loliguncula* Steenstrup, 1881

Thumbstall Squid
Loliguncula brevis (Blainville, 1823)

(after F. W. Lane, *Kingdom of the octopus* [New York: Sheridan House, 1960], p. 14)

(after G. L. Voss, *Bull. Marine Sci. Gulf & Caribbean* 5[2]:113 [1956])

Size: 75 mm.
Color: Cream with numerous reddish brown spots uniformly distributed over dorsal and ventral surfaces except for ventral surfaces of fins; narrow line down middle of back.
Description: Short and chunky with broad round fins about half length of body; tentacles long, slender with clublike ends; arms short, dorsal pair shortest.
Habitat: Bays and near shore; salinities of 17 to 30 ppt.
Localities: Entire.
Occurrence: Common.
Range: Maryland to Florida; Gulf of Mexico; Caribbean; South America to Río de la Plata.
Remarks: Moves out of bays to a few miles offshore during January and February; edible but primarily used for bait.

Genus *Loligo* Lamarck, 1798
Subgenus *Doryteuthis* Naef, 1912

Plee's Striped Squid
Loligo (Doryteuthis) pleii (Blainville, 1823)

(after Voss 1956, fig. b, p. 117)

Size: Up to 20.3 cm.
Color: Cream with long, narrow, wavy maroon lines running along side of mantle; small, maroon dots on remainder of mantle.
Description: Slender with large fins more than half of body length; males with large

reddish flame markings on under side of body; arms short; pen with straight, thickened sides.
Habitat: Offshore at depths of 13 to 46 meters (7 to 25 fathoms).
Localities: Entire.
Occurrence: Common offshore.
Range: Tropical waters from Bermuda and south Florida; Gulf of Mexico; Caribbean Sea; Guianas.
Remarks: Prefers salinities greater than 30 ppt. but often caught in trawls with *Loliguncula brevis; Loligo plealeii* Lesueur, 1821, better known than any loliginid squid; however, in northwest Gulf of Mexico generally found at depths of 37 to 183 meters (20 to 100 fathoms) with salinities greater than 33 ppt.

Order OCTOPODA Leach, 1817
Suborder INCIRRATA Grimpe, 1916
Family OCTOPODIDAE Orbigny, 1840
Subfamily OCTOPODINAE Grimpe, 1921

Genus *Octopus* Cuvier, 1797

Pygmy Octopus
Octopus joubini Robson, 1929

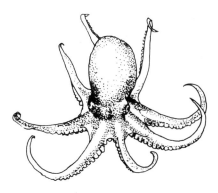

Size: 120 to 152 mm.
Color: Reddish brown with several large white pimples around eye.
Description: Small with short, relatively equal-length arms; mating arm of male has fairly large spoon-shaped organ at tip.

Habitat: Shallow water, sandy bottom to about 9 meters (5 fathoms).
Localities: South, west.
Occurrence: Fairly common.
Range: Georgia south to Gulf of Mexico; Caribbean to Guianas.
Remarks: Often lives in old clam shells; lifespan about 1 year.

Common Atlantic Octopus
Octopus vulgaris Lamarck, 1798

Size: 307–900 mm.
Color: Variable but commonly mottled reddish brown, white, and tan.
Description: Chunky with stout arms, upper pair always shortest; mating arm of male shorter with minute spoon-shaped organ at tip; may weigh 10 pounds.
Habitat: All types of bottom in shallow water to outer edge of continental shelf.
Localities: Entire.
Occurrence: Fairly common.
Range: Worldwide.
Remarks: Among rocks on jetties and sea walls; lives 1 or 2 years; males usually die following mating; females, after clusters of eggs, which it broods, are hatched.

Index

Index to Color Photographs

Striped False Limpet, C-13
Sunray Venus, C-23
Thick Lucina, C-18
Tiger Lucina, C-18
Tinted Cantharus, C-10
True Spiny Jewel Box, C-18
True Tulip Shell, C-11
Tulip Mussel, C-15
Turkey Wing, C-13

Virgin Nerite, C-2
Von Salis' Triton, C-9
White Crested Tellin, C-21
White Miniature Ark, C-14
White Wentletrap, C-4
Whitened Dwarf Olive, C-12
Yellow Cockle, C-19
Zebra Periwinkle, C-3